Practical Designs for Wood Turning

Practical Designs for Wood Turning

Roland Seale

Bell & Hyman

Published in paperback in 1985 by Bell & Hyman Limited, Denmark House,
37–39 Queen Elizabeth Street, London SE1 2QB

Reprinted in 1985

First published by Evans Brothers Limited in 1957
Reprinted 7 times

ISBN 0 7135 2563 0

Printed and bound in Great Britain at the
University Press, Cambridge

CONTENTS

v

Readers should see the companion volume, THE PRACTICAL WOOD TURNER by F. Pain. It is written specially for the beginner, and deals with the handling of tools, methods of chucking, and all the other problems that arise when turning.

FOREWORD

ONE OF THE many attractions of wood turning is the large variety of articles which can be produced with the aid of comparatively simple tools. The home craftsman will find many examples within his scope among the wide range of designs shown on the following pages. He will also find that much of the text is devoted to practical instructions on chucking and the turning methods which will best meet his requirements. The designs include both contemporary and period styles, and most of them are suitable also for quantity production for profit.

It may be said that craftsmanship and good design combine to improve the product. In many cases, however, it is no more difficult to make an article of good design than one which is bad or indifferent. Refinement does not necessarily imply complicated shape, and plain surfaces are not always improved by elaborate ornamentation. The designer's job is to guide the craftsman's hand and ensure that he makes the best use of his skill. In so doing he can often evolve objects of simpler form which combine fitness of purpose with pleasing appearance.

It is important to study the grain markings of hardwoods and allow them to provide natural adornment by employing bold curves. Subsequent carving and applied decoration can often with advantage be thereby avoided. Designs which embody these principles are equally suitable for mass production on automatic machines or for the home craftsman working with limited equipment.

ROLAND SEALE

PRACTICAL DESIGNS FOR WOODTURNING

I. HANDLES AND KNOBS

HANDLES FOR TOOLS and domestic uses are produced on the lathe in many shapes and sizes, and, although the modern automatic machine may give an irregular form more suitable for gripping, the plain circular handle remains the most general in use. Handles for chisels, gouges, etc., are usually made from beech, although boxwood is frequently used for better-class work.

TOOL HANDLES

Centering the work. As a simple example of turning between centres the methods employed in making a chisel handle are first dealt with in some detail as they will be applied later on to work of a more difficult character. Fig. 1 illustrates the various stages in making the turning chisel handle shown at (A) on Fig. 2. As the finished diameter is 1⅜ in. it should be made from material not less than 1⅝ in. square. The length required is about 8 in. The work-piece is first centred at each end by drawing the diagonals shown at (A), Fig. 1, and the intersection points lightly centre-punched. It is advisable, even on small diameters, to remove the corners of the square before commencing turning as this reduces vibration and tool wear. The maximum diameter of the finished work can if preferred be drawn on each end as a guide to the amount to be planed off as shown at (B), but this is not really essential.

The headstock spindle is fitted with a fork centre and the work-piece pushed on to it, making sure that the point engages with the centre-punch mark.

Now drive the forks into the wood by tapping the opposite end of the work with a mallet. Slide the tailstock along the bed until its centre engages with the second centre-punch mark. Lock the tail-stock to the bed and advance the spindle with the handwheel until the centre is firmly embedded in the work. Withdraw the centre

I

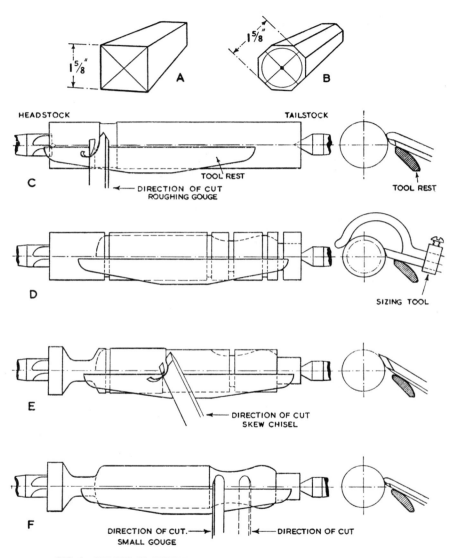

FIG. I. STAGES IN TURNING THE CHISEL HANDLE AT (A), FIG. 2

and apply a little vaseline to it. Re-engage the centre so that the work is just able to turn freely, and lock the spindle.

Roughing with the gouge. The first turning operation is to reduce the workpiece to a cylinder a little above the finished maximum diameter. The gouge is used for this purpose and it is

GROUP OF TOOL HANDLES IN VARIOUS WOODS
These are excellent practice. Such woods as beech, mahogany, walnut, rosewood, box, and lignum vitae can be used

held with the handle downwards at an angle of about 25 deg. from the horizontal. The height of the tool rest is set so that the cutting edge is well above the centre line as shown at (C), Fig. 1. Note also how the gouge is tilted towards the direction of the cut with the bevel tangential to the work. The first cut is made about 2 in. from one end and the tool moved sideways till it runs off the end. The diameter should be checked at this stage with the calipers set at $1\frac{1}{2}$ in.

The gouge is tilted in the opposite direction and a similar cut made at the opposite end. The centre portion is now reduced to the same diameter.

Cutting the sizing grooves. These grooves show the depth of

3

HANDLES AND KNOBS

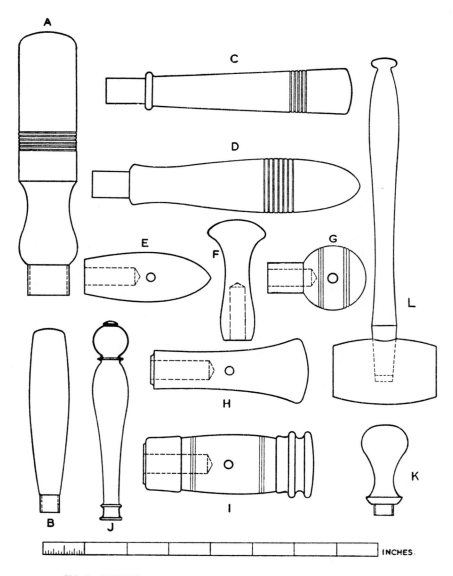

FIG. 2. VARIOUS HANDLES FOR TOOLS AND APPLIANCES, ETC.

cut at the main changes in section, the bottom of the grooves being the finished diameter of the handle at that point. The positions of these grooves are shown in the left-hand view at (D), Fig. 1. They are marked off with pencil and rule and, with the work rotated by hand and the pencil held on the tool rest, the marks are continued

TOOL HANDLE BEING TURNED BETWEEN CENTRES
The preliminary work is done with the gouge, and the chisel used to finish off

round the diameter so that they will be easily followed when the lathe is running. Sometimes the marks are made on the rest itself when the latter is of wood.

When many handles have to be made to the same pattern the position of the sizing grooves can be marked at the edge of a strip of wood, and this held against the revolving cylinder and the marks transferred.

The sizing grooves can be cut with a parting tool held in the right hand while the calipers, set to the required bottom diameter, are held against the work with the left hand. As the tool is advanced the calipers drop lower into the groove until they reach the centre when cutting is stopped.

An easier method is to employ a sizing tool like the one shown in the right-hand view at (D). This consists of a narrow chisel of rather deep section having a straight cutting edge. Attached to it by means of a clamp is a hook which engages with the back of the groove during cutting. The distance from the inside of the hook to the cutting edge is set to the required size of the finished groove. The tool is held on the work and pulled gently back towards the

TURNING A TOOL HANDLE
Note the ferrule slipped over the tail stock. It is thus easy to see whether it fits without removing the latter

operator to ensure that the hook is always in contact, while at the same time the tool is lowered until it ceases cutting.

Finishing operations. The major diameter is reduced to finished size with the skew chisel as shown at (E). The tool is placed on the rest with the bevel rubbing the work and gradually drawn downwards until the lower part of the cutting edge makes contact.. The chisel is also tilted towards the direction of the cut to prevent the top corner from digging in.

Now the small end next to the tailstock is turned to size. Some of the material should first be removed with a small gouge before finishing with a small skew chisel. The shoulder at the headstock end is cut in a similar manner. It now remains to form the centre

6

shape with a small gouge. This is held similarly to the large roughing gouge. The direction of the cuts is shown at (F), Fig. 1. Alternatively the shape can be scraped with a round-nosed chisel which requires much less skill in its manipulation than the gouge. The chisel is held flat on the rest and is inclined slightly downwards towards the work as at (A), Fig. 3, the cutting edge being approximately on the centre line of the work. The wood is removed by a scraping action. The resulting finish is inferior to that obtained with the gouge and it is most important that the tool is properly ground and kept really sharp.

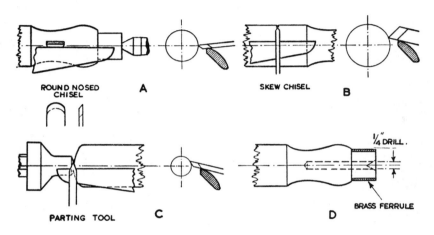

FIG. 3. STAGES IN TURNING BETWEEN CENTRES
A Scraping tool being used. B. Rings being cut. C. Use of parting tool. D. Drilling for tang

The six small V-grooves are made with the skew chisel resting on its edge with the acute point downwards as at (B), Fig. 3. The chisel must be held firmly and should slope upwards with the tool rest a little above centre. The work should now be examined to ensure that no tool marks remain and that the surface is free from blemishes, after which it is rubbed down lightly with glasspaper. Starting with a medium grade, the hand should be kept moving from side to side while the lathe is in motion. Fine glasspaper follows and a final polish given with a handful of shavings.

Parting off at the headstock end is the final operation in the lathe. This is performed with the V-pointed parting tool shown at (C), Fig. 3. The tool should not be allowed to cut right through the

7

work; it should be gently lowered until the bottom of the groove is about ¼ in. diameter. The end is cut off with a knife or a fine saw after removal from the lathe.

Most handles are provided with a brass ferrule, shown at (D), to prevent splitting when the tang of the tool is driven in. The ferrule is parted off from tubing and must be a tight fit on the handle.

Carving chisel. As a contrast to the first design the handle shown at (B), Fig. 2, is for a small carving chisel. After roughing out with the gouge and cutting the sizing grooves the handle is finished with the skew chisel starting from the centre and working outwards to each end. At (C) and (D) are two handles for general domestic purposes.

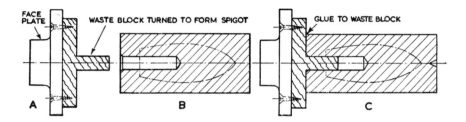

FIG. 4. USE OF FACE PLATE FOR TURNING A SHORT HANDLE

UMBRELLA HANDLES

Turning on the faceplate. Five types of turned umbrella handles are shown at (E, F, G, H, and I), Fig. 2. These could be turned between centres and the hole for the stem bored afterwards. A much better plan, however, is to employ a method which will ensure that the hole is truly concentric with the outside shape—a very necessary requirement in work of this kind. Three ways of achieving this are given in Figs. 4 and 5. The first is intended for those who have no equipment other than the faceplate.

Method 1. The faceplate must first be provided with a centering device as shown at A, Fig. 4. This is made from a suitable piece of waste hardwood screwed to the faceplate and turned down to leave a projecting spigot about 1 in. long, the diameter of which is the same as the umbrella stem. The workpiece shown at (B) is cut from square material, and one end centred by drawing the diagonals.

The longitudinal hole for the stem is drilled by hand taking care that it is reasonably in line with the axis. Countersink the hole slightly and chamfer the corners of the workpiece before mounting on the faceplate as shown at (C).

If it is found that the end of the workpiece is not square with the faceplate block it must be trued up by hand until a good fit is obtained. This is necessary because the two parts have to be glued together. When applying the glue care must be taken not to let any run on to the spigot or down the hole when assembling. The

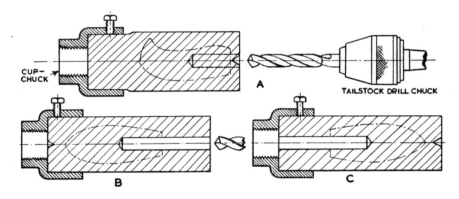

CUP-CHUCK

A

TAILSTOCK DRILL CHUCK

B

C

FIG. 5. ALTERNATIVE METHOD USING CUP CHUCK

faceplate can be removed from the lathe and the workpiece cramped in position until the glue has hardened.

In the first stages of turning the tailstock centre should be engaged, especially during the first roughing operation with the gouge. Cut the sizing grooves and withdraw the tailstock centre to allow the pointed end to be turned with the skew chisel, working from the maximum diameter down to the point. Reversing the chisel, start at the maximum diameter and work downwards to the opposite end. After finishing with glasspaper and polishing with a handful of shavings, the work may be parted off by cutting down to the spigot diameter.

Method 2. Cup chuck and tailstock drill chuck. This makes use of two useful pieces of equipment both of which are shown at (A), Fig. 5. The first is the cup chuck which is screwed on to the headstock spindle in the same manner as the faceplate.

9

HANDLES AND KNOBS

The chuck has a parallel bore, usually about 2 in. diameter, and the end of the workpiece is first turned down to fit tightly inside it. Several radial screws are provided which are tightened down on to the work to hold it securely. This chuck is made specially for wood-turning purposes and is preferable to the jaw type which relies on a high local pressure to grip the work. The jaws tend to bruise the wood badly, and an accidental tool dig-in may easily pull the work out of the chuck; also there is more risk of tool damage due to

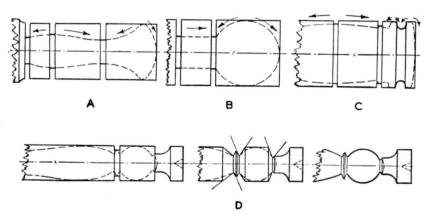

FIG. 6. PRELIMINARY SIZING GROOVES TO ENSURE ACCURACY

hitting the rotating jaws. The only requirement for the cup chuck is that it must not run out of truth. One word of caution, however: keep the knuckles clear of the projecting setscrews.

The tailstock centre may be used during the initial roughing operation with the gouge after which it is withdrawn and the centre removed ready for fitting the second piece of equipment, the drill chuck. This is provided with a Morse taper shank to fit the tailstock spindle and it is advanced to the required depth with the handwheel. For comparatively short holes the ordinary twist drill cuts quite well, and the results are the most accurate that can be produced in the lathe. It is not, however, so suitable for boring long holes as the parallel lands of the drill tend to bind in the hole. At a later stage the special methods employed for long holes will be described.

Referring again to the workpiece it will be seen that it is parted off at the radiused end of the handle in the design shown in dotted outline above the centre line. Where the handle has a pointed end, as in the first example shown below the centre line, it cannot be completely finished before parting. For this reason a third method is shown at (B) and (C).

Method 3. In this case both ends of the workpiece are turned down to fit the cup chuck. The hole for the stem is first drilled as at (B). The workpiece is then reversed in the chuck as at (C) so that the work can be turned from the opposite direction. See that the hole is running true before starting.

Having rough-turned the workpiece with the gouge it is now brought down almost to finished maximum diameter with the skew chisel and the appropriate sizing grooves cut. Three examples are shown at this stage in the diagrams (A, B, and C), Fig. 6. Note the small arrows indicating the direction in which the cuts are made when finishing the contours. For this purpose the small gouge is again used and held in the position shown in (F), Fig. 1. When cutting small radiused beads like those on the handle (I), Fig. 2, the gouge is manipulated as at (B), Fig. 7. As the cutting edge is rolled over the corner the handle of the gouge is moved towards the left in a continuous motion. The tool is then rolled in the opposite direction and the gouge handle moved to the right to cut the opposite side of the bead.

Materials and finish. The umbrella handles described above can be made from hardwood such as walnut, rosewood, box, syca-more, and so on. Ebony or coromandel would suit the ball-shaped handle (G), Fig. 2 and as an alternative handle (I) offers possibilities for a painted finish with the two ends in bright colours. As they have to withstand the weather, all the handles should be protected with a coat of varnish or clear cellulose lacquer.

FURTHER EXAMPLES

The remainder of the examples in Fig. 2 include the ornamental handle (J). This was made for a long brass toasting fork and was cut from beech, stained and french polished. For fine work of this kind a close-grained hardwood which cuts cleanly should be used. At (D), Fig. 6 are shown three stages in turning the end of this handle. The deep V-grooves can be made with the small skew chisel; this is held on its edge with the acute point downwards. The chisel handle is then slowly lowered to raise the point into the work. Care must be taken during this operation not to twist the chisel sideways or a dig-in will result. The groove is widened by making successive cuts on either side until the correct depth is reached after which the shapes can be completed with the small gouge.

Using the screw chuck. The small handle (K), Fig. 2, is for a rubber stamp. It is made from hardwood either painted black or left natural colour and varnished. Small articles of this kind, if required singly, can be turned on the screwpoint chuck. This has either a thread to suit the headstock spindle, or a Morse taper shank. The workpiece is screwed directly on to the plate and no further fixing is required. The arrangement is shown at (A), Fig. 7. It is advisable to drill a small hole in the wood before screwing in position; also provide a small recess at the centre to make sure that the work is pulled down flat on to the faceplate. When marking out remember to leave a space between the end of the screw and the end of the finished work to allow room for the parting tool.

When a number of similar small articles is required the cup chuck

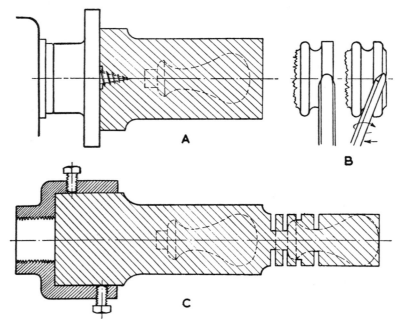

FIG. 7. ALTERNATIVE CHUCKING METHODS
A. Screw-point chuck. B. Turning beads. C. Cup chuck

12

may be used so that two or more can be turned from the same work-piece as shown at (C). The overhang of the work must not be too great and the tailstock centre should be used during the preliminary operations.

At (L), Fig. 2 is shown a small mallet or gavel which affords an example of a slender hardwood handle turned between centres.

CARVER'S MALLETS IN LIGNUM VITAE

After rough turning between centres the centre hole is bored. Turned plugs with spigots enable the turning to be completed between centres. The shaft runs right through and is wedged

13

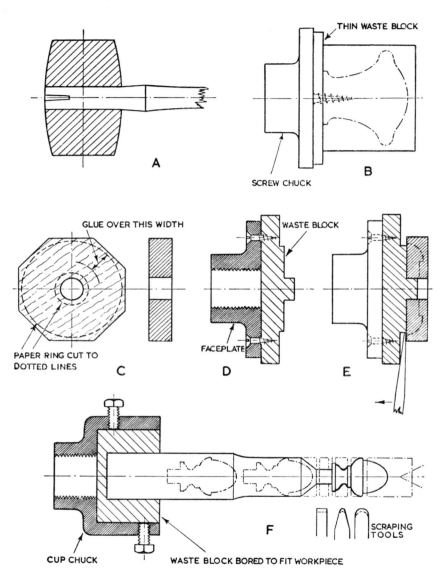

A

THIN WASTE BLOCK

SCREW CHUCK

B

GLUE OVER THIS WIDTH

PAPER RING CUT TO
DOTTED LINES

C

WASTE BLOCK

FACEPLATE

D

E

CUP CHUCK

WASTE BLOCK BORED TO FIT WORKPIECE

F

SCRAPING
TOOLS

FIG. 8. MALLET HEAD AND METHOD OF TURNING KNOBS
Note at (F) that, although the cup chuck is used the tail stock is necessary owing to the long
projection

14

Boxwood or rosewood is suggested for this article. The handle fits into the head by means of a taper shank which is glued in position. An alternative and stronger method of fixing handles of this type is shown at (A), Fig. 8. Here the handle is turned with a parallel shank the end of which is then sawcut and a taper wedge is driven in to fix the head. The handle must be made a good fit and the wedge positioned at right angles to the grain.

Carver's mallets. These were turned in lignum vitae, one with a shaft of beech and the other of purpleheart. Each head was rough turned between centres, and the hole for the shaft bored through from each side. The method of doing this was to hold the head against the tail stock point, start the bit at the centre, and run the lathe at a slow speed, gradually screwing the tail stock forwards and pressing back on the head to prevent grabbing. When reversed to complete the hole a small shouldered plug was turned to enable the work to be centred at the tailstock once again. Final turning was between centres with a pair of plugs. The shaft runs right through and is double wedged at the top, the end of the hole being opened slightly to allow for expansion.

TURNED KNOBS AND ROSES

Fig. 9 shows a selection of knob designs for various purposes all of which can be turned either in the cup chuck or on the screw chuck. One method is shown at (B), Fig. 8. Here the screw chuck is used and a thin piece of waste hardwood is first fitted so that the workpiece can be turned for its full length without the tools touching the faceplate. One end of the workpiece is trued up to form the finished end of the knob. As will be seen this method uses the minimum length of material and no parting off is necessary.

Roses. The grain of the wood should run lengthwise except in the case of the two roses for the door knobs (A and B), Fig. 9. These are made from material about $2\frac{1}{4}$ in. wide and $\frac{1}{2}$ in. thick, and one way of holding this type of work is shown in Fig. 8 (C, D, and E). The wood is first planed flat on one side and cut roughly to shape as at (C). The centre hole is drilled to the finished size, care being taken that it is square with the face. A waste piece of hardwood is now either mounted on the screw chuck or screwed to the faceplate and turned down to leave a small spigot which should be a good fit in the hole already drilled in the workpiece. The outside diameter is also reduced to a little below the finished size of the rose as at (D).

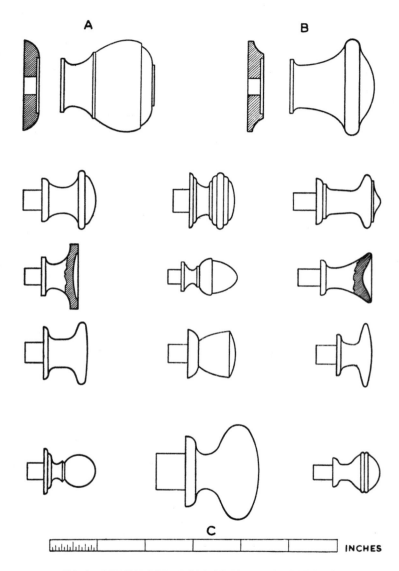

FIG. 9. DESIGNS FOR KNOBS SUITABLE FOR FURNITURE

At (E) is shown the method of attaching the work to the waste piece. The two are glued together with a piece of newspaper interposed between them so that they can be easily separated after turning. The paper will tear quite easily when the rose is prised off with a screwdriver as shown. The glue should extend about halfway across the face and time must of course be allowed for it to harden.

Knobs. Door knobs can be made from almost any hardwood stained as required and wax polished. Beech is a suitable material though oak and walnut will present more attractive grain effects. The table drawer knob (C) is provided with a spigot for gluing and should be in beech or birch.

The remainder of the examples are for cabinet doors and drawers and are applicable to many varieties of furniture styles. Small knobs of this sort are frequently made from beech stained after assembly to the individual cabinet finish. As it is almost certain that more than one will be required for a particular cabinet the most suitable method of turning is that shown at (F), Fig. 8. Again the cup chuck is used so that a number of parts can be produced at one setting. If the chuck is large in relation to the finished work diameter a great deal of timber will be wasted. To avoid this a hardwood block can be fitted into the chuck and bored out to receive the workpiece cut from dowelling or previously turned from square material. This must of course be a tight fit in the waste block and and can be glued in position to make a firmer fixing.

During the initial stages of turning the tailstock centre should be engaged. For fine work of this kind scraping tools have to be employed. These are all flat tools which are often ground from old files and held as already illustrated at (A), Fig. 3. They are often specially shaped to suit the contours of a particular part. Three such tools are shown at (F), Fig. 8.

Starting at the tailstock end the knobs are completely turned and parted off one at a time. During the final parting operation the knob should be held lightly in the fingers so that it can be grasped when it is free and not allowed to fly off into some obscure corner of the workshop.

USE OF THE GOUGE IN TURNING

ONE WAY OF HOLDING THE LONG-CORNERED CHISEL

2. KITCHEN ACCESSORIES

CABBAGE PRESSER AND POTATO MASHER

THE CABBAGE PRESSER (A), Fig. 1, is made in two parts. The handle, made from beech or sycamore, is turned between centres in a similar way to that described for the chisel handle in Fig. 1, page 2. It is provided with a large diameter spigot to fit tightly into the head. The material required for the head is a block about $5\frac{3}{4}$ in. square by $1\frac{1}{4}$ in. deep planed flat on one side to fit directly on to the faceplate. It is prepared as shown at (B). The two diagonals are drawn on the wood to mark the centre point and a diameter is struck equal to that of the face plate.

Chucking. Sketch (C) shows the set-up for the first turning operation. Note that the woodscrews enter only that part of the wood which will later be turned off. When fixing the block, the faceplate should be removed from the lathe spindle and the block clamped to it to prevent any movement while the holes are drilled and the screws inserted.

Scraping. Having replaced the faceplate the tool rest should be set a little below the centre of the work and in a suitable position to true up the outside diameter. This should first be roughed with the gouge and finished with a flat scraping chisel, the latter being held pointing slightly downwards.

For turning the face of the block, the tool rest must first be set parallel with it, a little below centre, and as close to the wood as possible. The round-nosed scraper chisel is used for roughing the face, the cut being started from the centre and continued to the edge. A flat scraper chisel is used for finishing. Many turners prefer to use scraping tools for all faceplate work and the correct position for holding the tools is shown at (E), Fig. 2. A steel rule held across the diameter will check the flatness of the face. The round-nosed scraper will form the radiused edge.

Centre hole. It now remains to bore the $1\frac{1}{8}$ in. diameter centre hole. If a tailstock chuck is available a machine twist drill may be used to drill a pilot hole. The tailstock spindle is advanced slowly and the depth of the hole carefully checked.

Another method is to use an ordinary brace and a Forstner bit. A small recess is first cut in the face to locate the bit. The brace

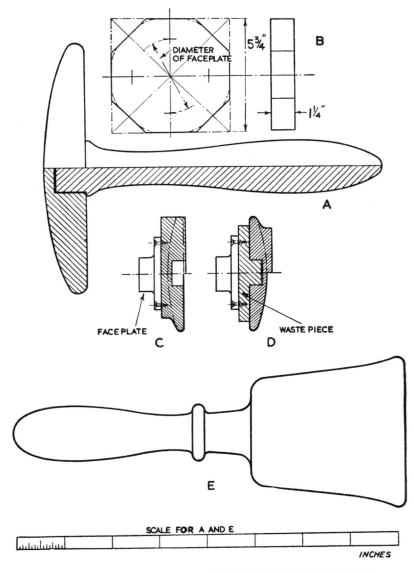

FIG. I. CABBAGE PRESSER AND POTATO MASHER IN SYCAMORE

is then held to the work with the right hand while the lathe is rotated slowly by the left hand or run at a slow speed—see (H), Fig. 2. A scraping tool is used to open out the hole to the correct size and care must be taken to keep the bore parallel.

To turn the opposite side of the head it is necessary to re-chuck

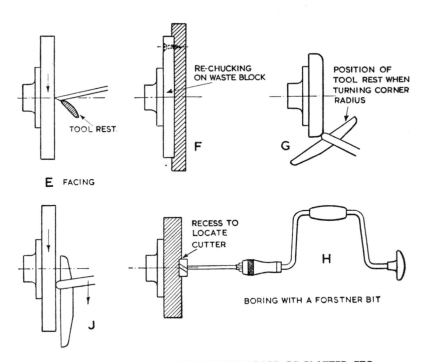

RE-CHUCKING ON WASTE BLOCK

POSITION OF TOOL REST WHEN TURNING CORNER RADIUS

TOOL REST.

E FACING

F

G

RECESS TO LOCATE CUTTER

H

BORING WITH A FORSTNER BIT

J

FIG. 2. METHOD OF TURNING BREAD BOARD OR PLATTER, ETC.

the work and this is done by turning a hardwood waste piece as shown at (D), Fig. 1. The spigot must be made a tight fit in the hole already bored, after which the head is driven into position with a mallet. Provided the faces are square and the spigot fit so tight that the work cannot be moved by hand, it is quite possible to turn the remainder of the work with scraping tools without having to resort to gluing the two pieces together with a paper insert. After final glasspapering and polishing the handle can be fitted into the head, a little glue having been applied to the inner end of the spigot.

KITCHEN ACCESSORIES

The potato masher shown at (E), Fig. 1 is turned between centres from a 3½-in. square block of beech. Most of the work can be done with the gouge though the handle calls for a little final shaping with scraper tools and the end face is also cut with the round-nosed chisel.

BREAD BOARDS

The bread board (A), Fig. 3 is 10 in. diameter. Work of this size requires either a lathe with a gap bed or alternatively a faceplate fitted on the outer end of the headstock so that the work is clear of the bed.

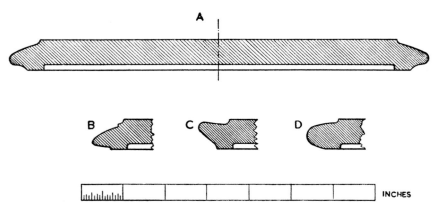

FIG. 3. SECTION THROUGH BREAD BOARD WITH ALTERNATIVE MOULDINGS

Chucking. Turned from beech the bread board can be made from material 1 in. thick by 11 in. square, but the problem is how to attach the workpiece to the faceplate without leaving screw holes in the top face. Thicker material could, of course, be used to enable the block to be screwed directly to the faceplate, the holes being eventually turned out when the block is reversed. To avoid such wastage of timber a piece of whitewood can first be screwed to the faceplate, turned to about 12 in. diameter, and faced.

The square workpiece is next planed flat on one side and fixed to the waste block with four screws, one at each corner outside the finished 10 in. diameter of the bread board. The screws should preferably be driven in from the back of the waste block. The face of the workpiece—which will form the underside of the bread

22

board—is now turned flat to give a finished surface a little over 10 in. diameter. The $8\frac{3}{8}$ in. diameter by $\frac{1}{8}$ in. deep recess is then turned, the work being carried out with the scraping tool, after which it can be finished with glasspaper and unscrewed.

The four corners are sawn off the workpiece, the screw holes being removed in the process. After further rough shaping the

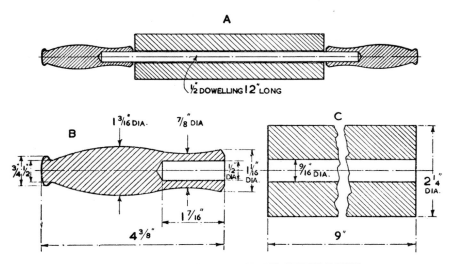

FIG. 4. ROLLING PIN REVOLVING ON CENTRE DOWEL

workpiece is ready for re-chucking to turn the top face and form the outer edge. To do this the waste block is first turned down to $8\frac{3}{8}$ in. diameter to locate the workpiece as shown at (F), Fig. 2. It is secured in position by four woodscrews. The holes left in the underside of the work can be filled afterwards with plastic wood or plugged. After turning, the top face is finished with glasspaper held over a flat rubber. Keep the hand moving backwards and forwards across the face while the lathe is running to prevent the glasspaper from leaving scratches. At (B, C, and D), Fig. 3 are alternative shapes.

ROLLING PINS

Two types of rolling pins are shown in Figs. 4 and 5. That at (A) Fig. 4 has a hole bored right through the roller to take a length of dowelling on which it rotates. It is always advisable to bore the hole first in such work as this, and as a preliminary the wood is planed to a square section leaving about $\frac{1}{8}$ in. to come off the flats during turning. The centre is then carefully marked.

Boring. The method shown at (A and B), Fig. 6 gives satisfactory results providing care is taken in the preparation of the simple jig which enables the boring to be done from each end. The support block and its guide are first planed, the height of the block being so arranged that the centre line of the workpiece coincides with that of the lathe spindle. The guide is screwed to the support block which is clamped to the lathe bed so that the centres again coincide at both ends.

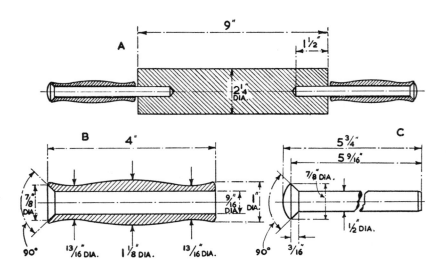

FIG. 5. ROLLING PIN WITH REVOLVING HANDLES

A taper shank drill chuck with a $\frac{9}{16}$ in. diameter drill is now fitted in the headstock spindle. It is essential that the drill runs true and that its cutting edge is properly ground. The work is advanced by means of the tailstock spindle, the centre producing a depression which will later serve as a guide for the drill when the workpiece is reversed. The hole must be bored a little over halfway through the block before reversing and this can be accomplished with the twist drill provided it is withdrawn frequently.

24

An alternative method is to first make a hole about 2 in. deep with the twist drill and bore the remainder with a parallel shank shell auger. This tool is like a gouge in section with a rounded end. These are usually sold with square shanks for use with hand tools. Many garages have a grinding machine on which the tool can be ground circular to fit the lathe chuck. Another way is to cut off the square portion of the shank and braze the tool to a short length of mild-steel bar. It is also possible to buy special deep boring tools which are not liable to wander in the wood.

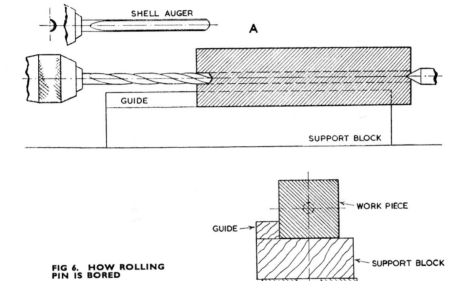

FIG 6. HOW ROLLING PIN IS BORED

Chucking. After boring, the corners of the block should be planed off and the work is ready for turning. For this a special fork centre may be used as shown at (A), Fig. 7. This is provided with a parallel centre which fits into the hole already bored. As this is unlikely to be available in the correct size an alternative method of centering can be used. First turn between centres the piece shown at (B), in which the centre portion is the same diameter as the hole in the workpiece. The centres must leave a good

25

impression so that the work can be accurately replaced in the lathe after the piece is cut in two and the halves fitted in each end of the work-piece as shown at (C) and (D). It will be necessary to glue the end taking the drive and this can be parted off down to the hole diameter after turning is completed.

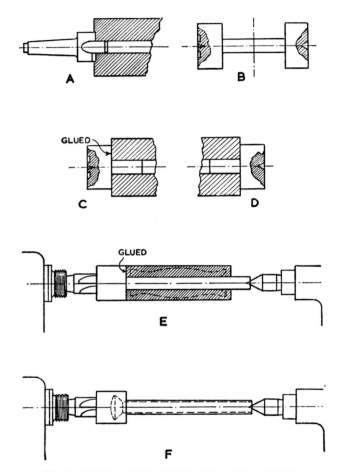

FIG. 7. DETAILS OF TURNING PINS AND HANDLES

Top (A) Special fork centre. (B) Method of turning plugs shown fitted at (C) and (D).
E. Handle turned on mandrel which is afterwards turned to form the pin

FIG. 8 (*opposite*). **ELEVATION AND PLAN OF TURNED STOOL**

INCHES

27

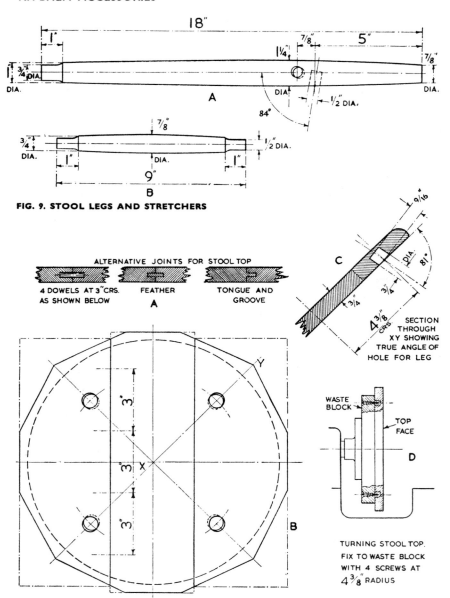

FIG. 9. STOOL LEGS AND STRETCHERS

ALTERNATIVE JOINTS FOR STOOL TOP

4 DOWELS AT 3"CRS.
AS SHOWN BELOW

FEATHER

A

TONGUE AND
GROOVE

C

SECTION
THROUGH
XY SHOWING
TRUE ANGLE OF
HOLE FOR LEG

WASTE
BLOCK

TOP
FACE

D

B

TURNING STOOL TOP.
FIX TO WASTE BLOCK
WITH 4 SCREWS AT
$4\frac{3}{8}$" RADIUS

FIG. 10. SEAT PLAN, AND METHOD OF JOINTING AND TURNING

Turning. For turning the roller the gouge is first used for roughing, working from the centre outwards to each end. This is followed by the skew chisel as described in Chapter 1.

In the second design (A), Fig. 5, the handles rotate on two turned pins and the roller has a $\frac{1}{2}$ in. hole bored $1\frac{1}{2}$ in. deep in each end. The handles (B) are turned after boring and they can be mounted between centres on the wood which will afterwards be used for making the pins in the manner shown at (E), Fig. 7. The pin is first turned $\frac{9}{16}$ in. diameter up to the shoulder at the headstock end and the handle, which must be a good fit on the pin, is glued at the shoulder end to take the drive. After turning is completed the handle is parted off at the shoulder end and the pin (C), Fig. 5, is then ready for turning as shown at (F), Fig. 7.

Rolling pins are nowadays made from beech, sycamore, or plane tree though at one time, when it was more plentiful, boxwood was often used.

A FOUR-LEGGED STOOL

The stool shown in Fig. 8 is made from beech and stands 18 in. high. Remembering that stools are often used for standing on as well as sitting on, the designer has made the top 12 in. diameter to ensure a reasonable foothold, and also provided four legs which give much greater stability than the usual three. The legs and stretchers are turned between centres, the dimensions being given in Fig. 9 (A and B). Note how the legs are shaped so that the thickest part is where the holes are bored for the stretchers. When boring the holes it must be remembered that the legs are handed as a result of one pair of stretchers being higher than the other.

Top. The top is shown made up of three pieces at (B), Fig. 10. This will come out of planed timber $4\frac{1}{4}$ in. wide by 37 in. long, the thickness being $\frac{7}{8}$ in. to allow for turning the top face. Three alternative ways of making the joints are shown at (A). After gluing together the corners should be removed and the top is ready for mounting on a waste block (D). To avoid having to fill up the screw holes the four screws fixing the top to the waste block can be positioned at the same radius as the holes which will later be bored to receive the legs.

3. CANDLESTICKS AND ELECTRIC TABLE LAMPS

FOR HUNDREDS OF years wooden candlesticks have been used for both domestic and ceremonial purposes. In some of the earlier ones no socket was provided, the candle being retained on a spike or "pricket".

SMALL CANDLE HOLDERS

The examples shown in Fig. 1 (A to F) are small domestic designs mainly for decorative purposes. They are all provided with a tightly fitting brass socket to afford some protection for the wood should the candle be allowed to burn too low. The socket should be made $\frac{27}{32}$ in. internal diameter to suit a standard $\frac{13}{16}$ in. diameter candle.

The two simplest types (A and C) are suitable for a painted or enamelled finish and can be made from any sound timber. Both will look effective if painted in two contrasting colours, with the base in the lighter shade. The top portion is turned separately in the cup chuck, and it is provided with a 1 in. diameter spigot to fit into the base. A piece of $\frac{1}{2}$ in. thick planed board will be required for the base which can be turned on the faceplate and bored to receive the spigot, the two parts being afterwards glued together. Alternatively, both designs may be turned from the solid in which case the screw chuck would be used leaving one hole only in the bottom face to be filled after turning.

Alternative designs. Two examples of modern styling (B and E), Fig. 1 have bold curves to display the grain pattern. These are made from hardwood with a waxed or french-polished finish. Suitable materials are walnut, Japanese oak, or mahogany. These can be turned on the screw chuck, the bottom face having first been planed flat.

The same methods and materials are suggested for the two traditional designs (D and F). Here most of the work will have to be done with scraping tools and light cuts are required, especially in the case of the tulip shape (F) where the stem is relatively weak.

As something of a novelty the author has shown at (G), Fig. 1 a candlestick he made some years ago which may serve as a useful exercise for the beginner. The workpiece was first screwed to the

30

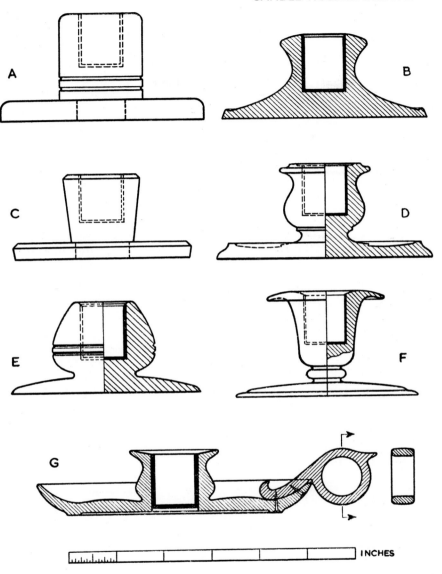

FIG. I. DESIGNS FOR SMALL CANDLE HOLDERS WITH SCALE

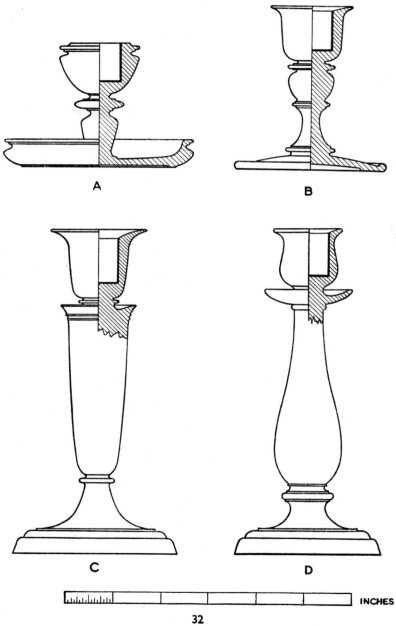

A

B

C

D

INCHES

faceplate and the underside finished. The centre hole 1 in. diameter. was bored right through and checked with the calipers to make sure that it was parallel. A waste piece with a spigot about 1½ in. long and 1 in. diameter was next turned up on the faceplate. The diameter of the spigot was carefully reduced until it was a tight fit in

TABLE LAMP TURNED IN MAHOGANY

FIG. 2 (left). DESIGNS FOR CANDLESTICKS

33

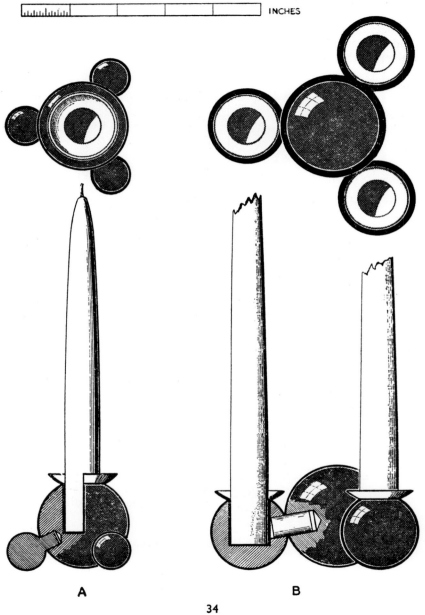

INCHES

A

B

34

the hole already bored in the workpiece. The latter was driven on to the waste block with the base towards the faceplate and the remainder of the turning completed. The handle was made from $\frac{1}{2}$ in. wood with a hole bored $\frac{13}{16}$ in. diameter, the remainder being cut out on a jig saw and rounded at the edges. It was fixed to the candlestick with screws, though a better method would be to dowel and glue the parts together.

For those who wish to try their skill on a more elaborate design the two candlesticks (A and B), Fig. 2 will give plenty of scope. They are both turned from solid blocks and much fine work with scraping tools is required to form the delicate shapes of the stems.

TWO PEDESTAL CANDLESTICKS

Two pedestal designs are shown at (C and D), Fig. 2. Although these are not actual copies they have something in common with the work of 18th-century craftsmen. Both examples are turned between centres and the wood used must be well seasoned and free from knots, cracks, or other obvious imperfections. If a piece of dry old oak is obtainable this would serve admirably. Walnut or mahogany are also suitable. As candlesticks of this type are mostly made in pairs a template of the contours should be cut from cardboard so that they can be readily checked.

BALL-TYPE CANDLE HOLDERS

In complete contrast with the previous designs the two modern styles (A and B), Fig. 3 consist entirely of ball shapes. In the first example the central ball carries the candle in a brass socket turned with an integral drip pan. The three balls forming the feet are turned with spigots which fit tightly into holes spaced 120 deg. apart in the central ball. These holes should be arranged so that the central ball is just clear of the table when the feet are finally glued in position. This will ensure that the weight is carried evenly on the three feet and there will be no tendency for the holder to rock. The feet could with advantage be made a little larger in diameter if a tall candle is to be used.

For turning the feet the method shown at (F), Fig. 8, page 14, can be used. The grain must run lengthwise on the spigot

FIG. 3 (left). BALL CANDLE HOLDERS FINISHED WITH PAINT

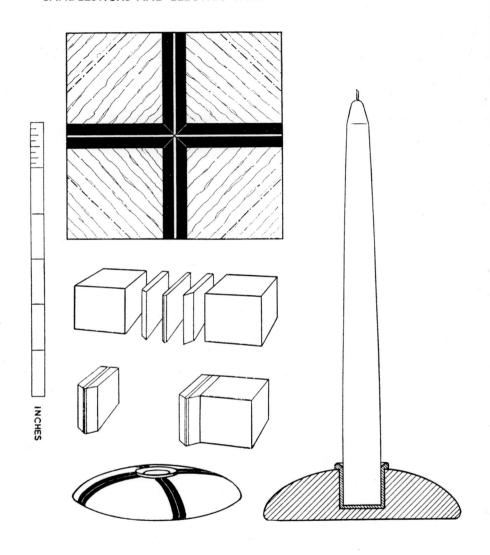

INCHES

FIG. 4. CANDLE HOLDER BUILT UP IN CONTRASTING WOODS

otherwise the foot may be broken off. The central ball can be turned and bored in the cup chuck.

Triple candlestick. The triple candlestick (B) is of similar construction except for the method of dowelling the four parts together. Here three separate dowels are used to enable the candle holders to be turned and bored in the cup chuck.

Although these two designs would look quite attractive if made from hardwood and finished by polishing, they are intended primarily for painted finishes.

LAMINATED CANDLE HOLDER

The last example, Fig. 4, is a small candle holder build up of a number of laminations, which can be made from small off-cuts, the wood being chosen to give a contrasting colour pattern. Four square blocks are first cut from light-coloured timber, such as sycamore or maple, with the grain running in the direction shown in the upper view. The two inner faces of each block must be flat and truly at right angles to one another so that they all fit together with no gaps showing.

Eight pieces of dark timber such as walnut, mahogany, coromandel, etc. are next prepared. These should be about $\frac{3}{16}$ in. to $\frac{1}{4}$ in. thick. The remaining four centre laminations are $\frac{1}{16}$ in. thick and should be of the same material as the four blocks. Note the mitres on the inner edge of the laminations which are required to produce a continuous surface on the underside of the candle holder. The sketches show the stages in which the pieces are assembled and glued together. They must be firmly clamped until the glue has hardened after which the workpiece can be turned in the usual way.

ELECTRIC TABLE LAMPS

Baluster design. Fig. 5 is the first of a number of table lamp designs, all of which require a long hole bored through the stem to accommodate the electric light flex. Because of this the beginner may at first be deterred from undertaking the work. It is possible to avoid the boring altogether by making the stem from two length of material glued together on the vertical centre line after a half-round groove has been cut down the centre of each joint face. This is not suitable for the first example where a continuous grain pattern is essential and the stem should be made from a solid length of the hardwood. The design calls for timber with a rich warm colouring as for instance the darker shades of walnut or mahogany.

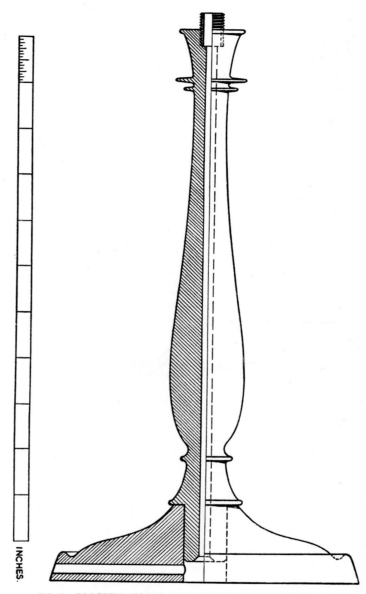

INCHES.

FIG. 5. GRACEFUL TABLE LAMP OF THE BALUSTER TYPE

Centre hole. The centre hole must be bored through the stem before any turning is started and with some care and patience this can be accomplished in the manner shown at (A) and (B), Fig. 6, page 25, using a $\frac{1}{4}$ in. diameter drill. A less professional method which the author has used, and which may appeal more to the amateur, consists of drilling a $\frac{9}{32}$ in. hole 3 in. to 4 in. deep in each end and following up with a long $\frac{1}{4}$ in. drill, the workpiece being again supported as shown on page 25. If the $\frac{1}{4}$ in. drill eventually binds in the hole it can be replaced with a still smaller one—say $\frac{7}{32}$ in.

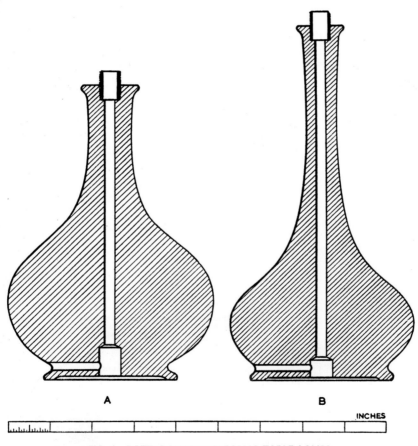

A   B

INCHES

FIG. 6. BOTTLE-SHAPED ELECTRIC TABLE LAMPS

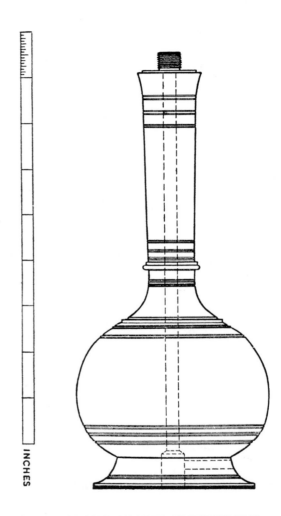

INCHES

FIG. 7. TABLE LAMP ON LINES OF PERSIAN VASE

diameter—also worked from each end with the lathe running at a slow speed until the centre is reached. The resulting hole may not be absolutely straight. It may require a little cleaning out where the holes meet or rather do not quite meet at the centre, but it is unlikely that a serious run-out will develop and providing the flex can be passed through easily no one will be any the wiser. The transparent plastic flex now on the market is much easier to thread through long holes than the older cotton-covered variety.

Special boring auger. The most satisfactory way is to use the special boring auger and back centre fitting made by several lathe manufacturers. In this the back centre is hollow and has a ring rather than a point. This enables the auger to be passed right through without wandering.

Turning the stem. After boring, the stem is turned between centres and a $\frac{7}{8}$ in. diameter spigot left at bottom end for fitting into the separate base. The upper end of the stem is bored out $\frac{15}{32}$ in. diameter by $\frac{3}{8}$ in. deep and a threaded brass tube $\frac{1}{2}$ in. diameter by $\frac{3}{4}$ in. long is screwed into the wood with half its length projecting to accept a standard electric light fitting. These threaded tubes can be obtained from any electrical dealer and the light fitting may be had with or without an integral switch as desired. Special fittings are also made with a coarse thread at one end to fit into the wood.

Base. The turning of the base should not present much difficulty. It can be screwed directly to the faceplate and finished at one setting if the bottom face is first planed flat. The central hole must be a tight fit on the stem spigot to which it is finally glued. The cross hole for the flex can be drilled by hand and a piece of green baize should be glued to the bottom of the lamp to prevent any damage to polished surfaces on which it may stand.

The surface finish on articles of this sort is very important and all traces of tool marks must be removed before applying wax or french polish.

The two examples in Fig. 6 are turned from solid blocks and they depend entirely on the grain pattern of the timber for effect. A variety of hardwoods could be used for these pieces. A light shade of oak is probably the most attractive; African walnut, mahogany, and haldu will also give pleasing results if a suitable block can be obtained. Wax polish should be applied to give a matt finish in preference to the brilliant appearance obtained by french polishing.

Persian vase. Modelled on the lines of a bronze Persian vase, the lamp shown in Fig. 7 is also turned from a single block of hard-wood. The surface is relieved with shallow grooves and a close-grained wood should be used which can afterwards be stained.

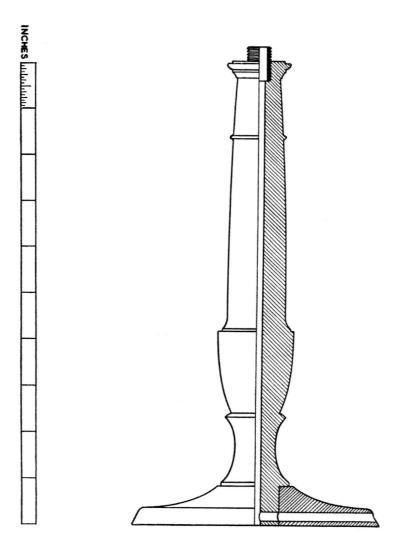

INCHES

FIG. 8. TABLE LAMP DESIGNED ON TRADITIONAL LINES

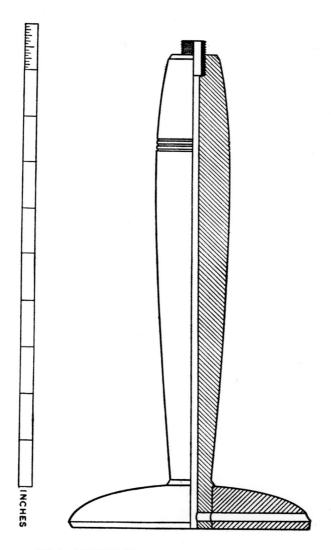

INCHES

FIG. 9. MODERN STYLE LAMP WITH CLEAN LINES

Sycamore is one wood which takes various coloured dyes very well, among them being dark green and grey which would suit the present design. Beech is also a wood which stains well. Either water or spirit wood stains may be used and they can be bought ready-made from the paint dealers.

Traditional design. The lamp in Fig. 8 is reminiscent of 18th century candlestick designs.

Modern style. The last example, Fig. 9, shows a contemporary "streamline" table lamp, the plain stem being relieved only by three shallow grooves at the upper end. Walnut is again the suggested material. If a lighter wood is preferred sycamore could be used.

PART FINISHED LAMP TO BE CARVED AND GILT

In turning a piece of this kind allowance has to be made for the carved detail

SUITABLE FOR THE NURSERY
The whole thing has a painted finish which gives a realistic appearance

45

4. CLOCK AND BAROMETER CASES

THE TWO SIMPLE designs in Fig. 1 are for the type of clock movement in which the frame is carried on the dial plate, the latter being provided with suitable brackets for fixing to the inside of the case. The case must be bored to fit the bezel holding the glass, and the back is closed with the usual metal plate secured by woodscrews so giving easy access to the movement. Both cases should be turned on the faceplate from a solid block; oak, walnut, or mahogany finished with french polish are suitable for the plain cylindrical case in the upper view. Here the feet are located in two shallow grooves cut in the periphery and they are attached by a single dowel glued in position as shown. This should be positioned in the centre of the foot.

Alternative design. The lower view shows a part-spherical case which calls for different treatment. Here the clock stands on four balls which are provided with integral spigots for fitting into four holes drilled radially in the case. It is most important that these holes are accurately positioned.

The best way to tackle problems of this kind is to construct a simple jig such as that shown in Fig. 2. Here a block of waste wood is turned to fit the bore in the clock case and the ends faced until the length is also the same as the case depth. A taper block is prepared to tilt the work to the correct angle. The base board to which the two parts are screwed is also provided with a vertical hardwood block having a hole bored through it to form a guide for the drill. This hole must be parallel to the base board and the height carefully measured so that its centre line coincides with the centre point of the case as shown. This centre line should be drawn across the top face of the turned block and the position of the two sets of holes for the feet marked on both ends of the case.

The work can be mounted on the jig and rotated until the marks are opposite to the centre line drawn on the block. To drill the remaining two holes it is only necessary to reverse the work and proceed as before. During the drilling operation the work can either be held by hand or (preferably) by a simple clamp screwed to the top of the jig. The success of this method depends largely on the accurate turning of the case. To make sure that this is spherical a template locating from the vertical face should be used.

46

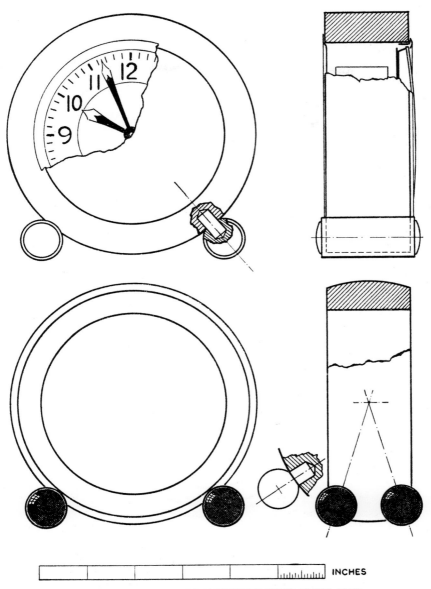

FIG. I. SIMPLE CASE FOR MOVEMENT WITH METAL FACE

INCHES

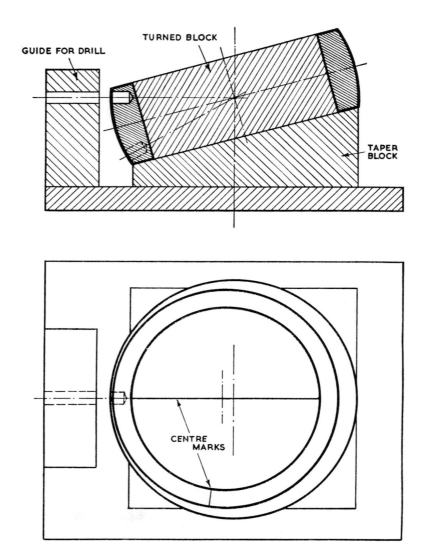

GUIDE FOR DRILL

TURNED BLOCK

TAPER BLOCK

CENTRE MARKS

FIG. 2. METHOD OF BORING HOLES TO TAKE FEET OF CLOCKCASE

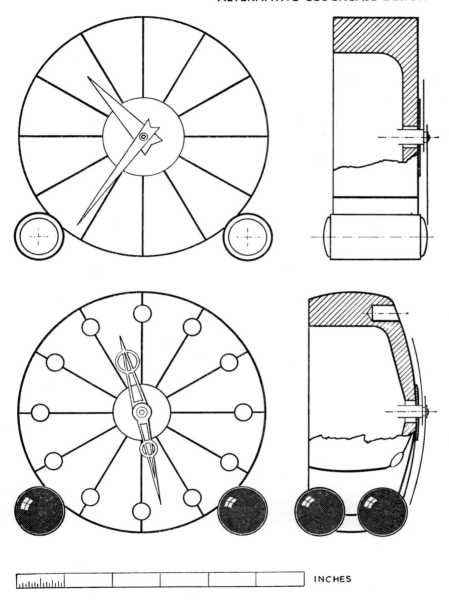

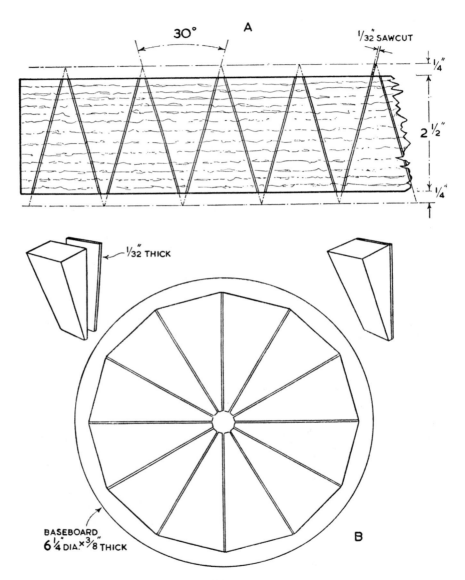

FIG. 4. PREPARING SECTORS FOR CLOCKCASES IN FIG. 3

BUILT-UP CLOCK CASES

The two clock cases in Fig. 3 are both built up from twelve sectors made from light-coloured hardwood such as sycamore. The sectors are separated by thin strips of dark wood, such as walnut, to provide the five-minute divisions on the face. In the first design plain cylindrical shapes are employed and there are no other markings on the face. This styling suits a clock movement with plain tapering hands like those illustrated.

Cutting the sectors. The sectors are produced from a planed-up block by cutting to the angles shown at (A), Fig. 4. The thickness of the block should be 2 in. for the first design and $2\frac{1}{2}$ in. for the second. A strip of the dark wood is next glued to one side of each sector and the parts are ready for assembly on a base board. This can be turned from plywood or from waste hardwood. The top face of the board has a sheet of white paper glued to it which is afterwards marked out as at (A), Fig. 5, to ensure that the sectors are correctly positioned.

The underside of the base must also be marked out as shown at (C), Fig. 5 so that the assembly can later be located accurately on the faceplate for the initial turning operation, and for this reason the markings on top and bottom must be truly concentric. Each segment, as it is glued to the base board and to its neighbour, must be separately clamped between its top face and the underside of the base, making certain that the vertical faces are firmly in contact over the entire surface. For this purpose twelve clamps are required. The completed assembly is shown at (B), Fig. 4.

Chucking. When the glue has thoroughly set the work is ready for mounting on the faceplate as shown at (A), Fig. 6. The markings on the underside of the base board are carefully lined up with the faceplate diameter before drilling the pilot holes for the woodscrews. After replacing the faceplate rotate the lathe and check that the face of the block is correctly positioned so that the five-minute divisions radiate from the centre. The precautions taken should ensure this, but should there be any error due to misplacement of the sectors during assembly it can be corrected by measuring the amount and direction of the discrepancy and repositioning the work on the faceplate. It is on account of the necessity for concentricity that the method of double re-chucking shown at (B and C), Fig. 6 is advocated. The accurately centred outer face of the workpiece at (A) thereby becomes the face of the case.

After turning the $3\frac{5}{8}$ in. diameter spigot the work is removed from the faceplate and the base board gently prised off with a chisel. A

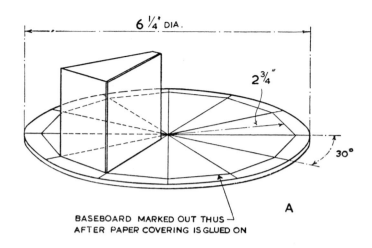

BASEBOARD MARKED OUT THUS
AFTER PAPER COVERING IS GLUED ON

A

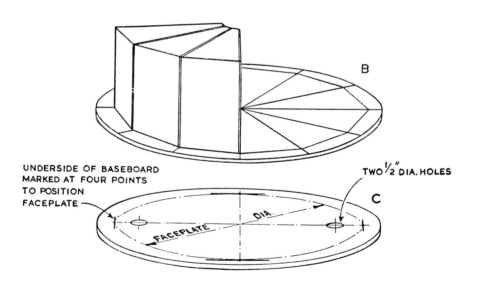

B

UNDERSIDE OF BASEBOARD
MARKED AT FOUR POINTS
TO POSITION
FACEPLATE

TWO ½" DIA. HOLES

C

FIG. 5. METHOD OF ASSEMBLING SECTORS, AND HOW WOOD IS CENTRED

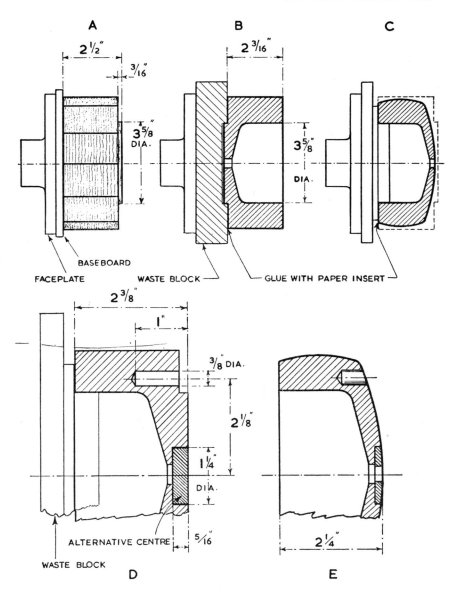

FIG. 6. STAGES IN TURNING (A, B, C), AND HOW PLUGS ARE INSERTED

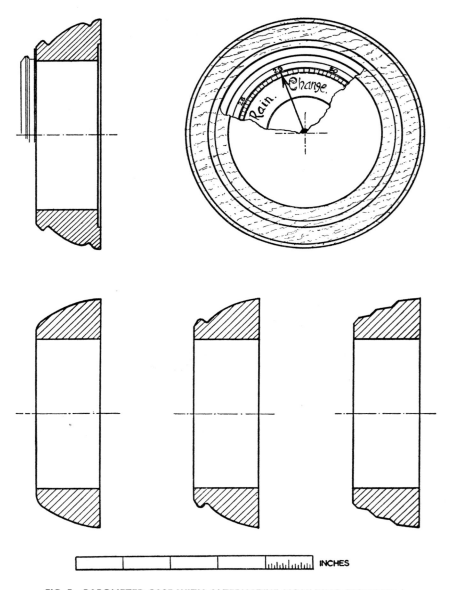

INCHES

FIG. 7. BAROMETER CASE WITH ALTERNATIVE MOULDING SECTIONS

waste piece is next turned up to fit the spigot and the workpiece glued in position with paper inserted after which the back face can be turned and the bore finished. For the final turning (C) the waste piece is turned down to fit the bore and the work is again glued with paper between the faces.

In the second design the face is relieved by fitting twelve plugs cut from a contrasting coloured hardwood on the five-minute divisions. These should be glued in the holes drilled in the position shown at (D), Fig. 6 which also shows an alternative method of finishing the centre with a dark-coloured hardwood insert. The plugs and the insert are glued in position before the final turning at (E). The ball feet, also in dark-coloured hardwood, are turned with spigots and fitted in a similar manner to those in Fig. 1. The holes for these can be drilled on the jig shown in Fig. 2.

BAROMETER CASES

The simple designs shown in Fig. 7 are for small barometer movements with a key slot in the metal backplate for hanging on the wall. They can be produced from any offcuts of hardwood stained and french polished.

SMALL CANDLE HOLDER. SEE DESIGN (G), PAGE 31

5. BOWLS AND DISHES

WOODEN BOWLS MADE from beech or sycamore have for centuries
been used for the preparation of food and the serving of meals.

TURNING A 9 INCH DIAMETER BOWL

At (A), Fig. 1 is a mixing bowl originally intended for chopping
suet, etc. for which purpose a knife with a semicircular blade was
provided.

Chucking. The bowl may be turned on the screw chuck, as
shown in Fig. 2 (A and B), providing the chuck has four holes for
additional wood screws to hold the work more securely. It is too
large to be held by the centre screw only. The advantage of the
centre screw is that it provides means of easily re-chucking the
work for turning the inside shape.

This method of re-chucking can, of course, be used only when

GROUP OF SMALL TURNED BOWLS IN VARIOUS WOODS

56

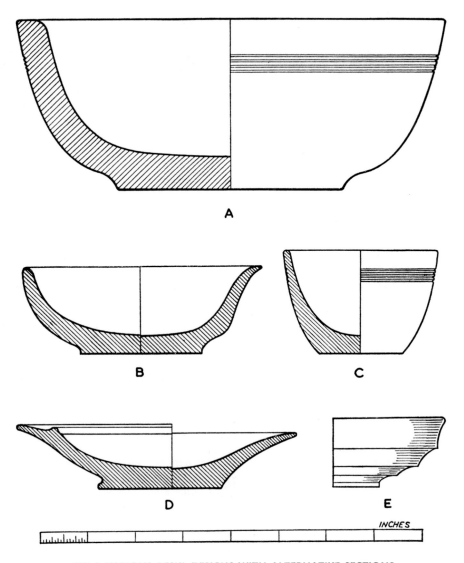

A

B

C

D

E

INCHES

FIG. I. VARIOUS BOWL DESIGNS WITH ALTERNATIVE SECTIONS

the bowl has a fairly thick base. The screw holes left in the bottom face can afterwards be plugged or filled with plastic wood.

The work piece should be cut roughly to a circular shape and one face planed flat with a small recess at the centre before mounting on the chuck as shown at (A), Fig. 2. The grain must, of course, run across the face of the block. The outside shape is first cut with the gouge, and the bottom finished slightly concave, after which it is glass-papered and polished. Before removing for re-chucking a small centre hole is cut in the bottom as shown. At (B) the bowl is shown reversed, the centre hole having positioned it accurately on the chuck. Again the four additional screws are used for holding the bowl firmly to the plate.

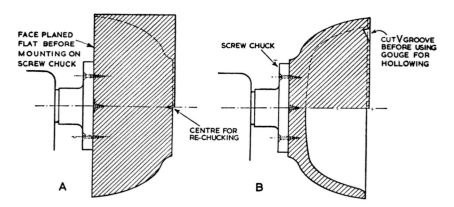

FIG. 2. ONE METHOD OF CHUCKING AND REVERSING BOWL FOR TURNING

Centre and screw holes show beneath

Turning the inside. Some material can be removed from the inside with the gouge; but it is advisable to first cut a groove near the inside edge as indicated. This provides a surface for the bevel of the gouge to rest on when starting the cut, and reduces the risk of the tool digging in and spoiling the top face. The groove can be cut with a chisel held flat on the tool rest which has been fixed parallel to the face being worked on and slightly below centre.

The inside surface is finished with a round-nosed scraper and it is as well to make a cardboard template of the contour so that the shape can be easily checked. After smoothing with glasspaper the bowl should be rubbed with handfuls of shavings to remove any remaining scratches.

SMALL BOWLS

At (B), Fig. 1 are two alternative shapes of small bowls for sweets or nuts. These can be made from a variety of hardwoods such as walnut, oak, or rosewood. These are turned on the faceplate as shown at (A and B), Fig. 3. After roughly shaping, the workpiece

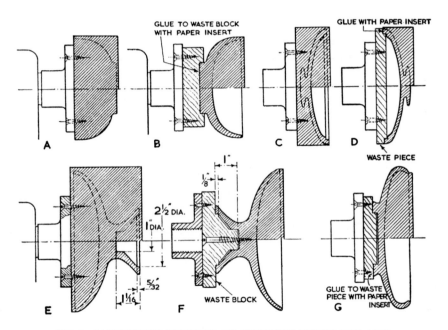

FIG. 3. ALTERNATIVE METHODS OF CHUCKING BOWLS AND LIDS

The use of a waste piece with spigot avoids screw holes at the underside

is screwed to the faceplate to enable the outside to be turned, the screws entering that part of the wood which will later be removed in the hollowing operation.

Reversing. For re-chucking, the bowl can be fixed to a waste block on the short parallel portion of the base, the two parts being glued together with a paper insert. The recess in the wasteblock

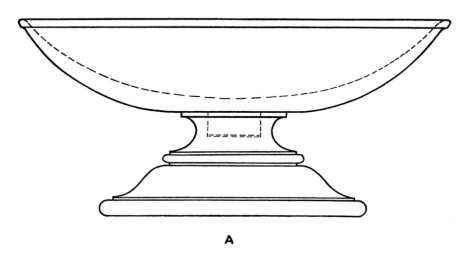

A

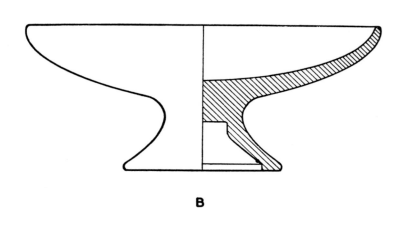

B

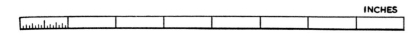

INCHES

FIG. 4. PEDESTAL BOWLS; A IS TWO-PART; B, SINGLE PIECE

is turned to a close fit with the square part. For turning the inside the round-nosed scraping tool is again used. After final polishing the bowl can be prised off the spigot and the bottom face cleaned up by hand.

Alternative designs. The small bowl shown at (C), Fig. 1 can be turned from a short length of hardwood 2½ in. square held in the cup chuck, the grain in this case running lengthwise. The base of the bowl is towards the headstock so that all the turning operations

BOWL OF SYCAMORE SANDWICHED BETWEEN MAHOGANY

can be carried out without re-chucking before parting off at the base.

The flat dish for nuts or sweets shown at (D), Fig. 1 in alternative designs can be turned on a small screw chuck providing the base is left thick enough to clear the end of the screw.

The design at (E) looks well. Note that the wood is first turned to a fair curve, and the hollows put in afterwards. Scraping is essential for finishing. If only fine cuts are taken and the tool kept sharp it is possible to avoid teasing out the grain at the two opposite parts where working against the grain is unavoidable.

PEDESTAL BOWLS

Two examples of pedestal bowls are given in Fig. 4. The first, (A), has a classical design of base which is made separate from the bowl, the two parts being spigoted and glued together. The block for the bowl is first prepared and screwed to the faceplate. The outside shape and the projecting $1\frac{1}{2}$ in. diameter spigot are finished and the work removed from the lathe. Now the block for the base is screwed to the faceplate after planing the bottom face true. The block is turned, the first roughing cuts being made with the gouge. Scraping tools should be used to form the small curves, and finally

BUILT-UP AND INLAID BOWL MADE ENTIRELY ON LATHE

The building-up of the bowl in two woods presents no difficulty. It is similar to the other built-up designs. For the lid inlay, however, a recess is turned in the oak to receive a sycamore disc. After gluing in this sycamore is recessed for the dark cocus inlay, leaving a narrow sycamore line.

When turning the inlay discs the grain must run crosswise. If the back centre is used several discs can be turned in one length and parted off. Each disc can be *slightly* tapered. Bore the holes for the sycamore inlays, putting a forstner bit in the 3-jaw chuck and offering the wood up to it. When the sycamore has been glued in the process can be repeated for the small tulip wood inlays. Finally, the whole thing is finally turned. If practicable it is an advantage after the preliminary turning of the lid to shape and making the recesses to keep the wood fixed to the face plate as there is then no difficulty about re-centreing.

the $1\frac{1}{2}$ in. diameter hole is bored a little deeper than the projecting spigot on the upper portion.

A good fit must be obtained between the two parts which are glued together while the base remains screwed to the faceplate. The glue should extend down the spigot and across the top face. While the glue is setting the tailstock can be brought up and the spindle tightened on to the top face of the bowl to provide the necessary pressure.

Allow plenty of time for the glue to set. It is a good plan to leave the work in position overnight, after which the final operation of turning the inside of the bowl can be carried out. Start first with a V-groove near the outer edge as described earlier in this chapter and take light cuts with the gouge and finish the shape with the scraper.

Modern design. The second bowl (B), Fig. 4 is a modern design made in one piece. The suggested method of turning this is shown on Fig. 3 (E and F). The outside is first turned with the block screwed directly to the faceplate. Next the bottom of the pedestal is hollowed out leaving two parallel recesses which will later be used for re-chucking purposes. After finishing the outside the work is removed from the lathe and a hardwood waste block screwed to the faceplate. This is turned to the shape shown at (F), the two spigots fitting accurately in the pedestal recesses. A hole is bored through the centre using the tailstock chuck.

The faceplate with the waste block still fixed in position is removed from the spindle so that a large wood screw may be inserted and screwed firmly into the centre of the bowl. The hole should first be countersunk by hand to receive the screw head. The assembly can now be replaced on the lathe spindle to enable the inside of the bowl to be turned. The double spigot is provided to give better support for the workpiece, most of the side load from the tool being taken on the two diameters while the centre screw provides the drive. As heavy cuts should obviously be avoided it is advisable to carry out most of the hollowing work with the scraping tool.

Materials and finish. In choosing material for work of this kind the following points should be borne in mind. Wood with a tendency to warp or split after turning must be avoided. Although well-seasoned timber should, of course, always be used for articles of turnery, special care in selection is essential with large-diameter work of comparatively thin section, otherwise it may be ruined by subsequent distortion. A well-figured grain is desirable to enrich the large plain surfaces. The wood must take a high surface finish. It is a good plan to rough turn bowls, and leave for as long as possible to dry out. After re-chucking the finished shape can be turned.

FURTHER EXAMPLES

All the examples in Fig. 5 have an internal recess in the base for re-chucking, and the method of gluing to the waste piece is shown at (G), Fig. 3. Care must be taken to see that the glue does not run down to the spigot or removal will be difficult. The covered bowl (A) is made from walnut. As a centre piece for the dressing table this design can serve as a powder bowl, jewel box, or container for toilet miscellanea.

It requires a different method of re-chucking. Here the roughly shaped block is screwed to the faceplate and the whole of the inside shape turned first as (C), Fig. 3. For re-chucking a waste piece is turned up with a spigot to fit inside the recess and the lid is secured in position again by a paper ring glued on both sides. The outside can now be turned and finished with wax or french polishing.

The fruit bowl (B), Fig. 5 can be made from European walnut and the smaller sweet bowls (C) from oak or walnut. Two alternative shapes are shown for the flat bowl (D), also made in walnut.

SHALLOW BOWL IN MAHOGANY

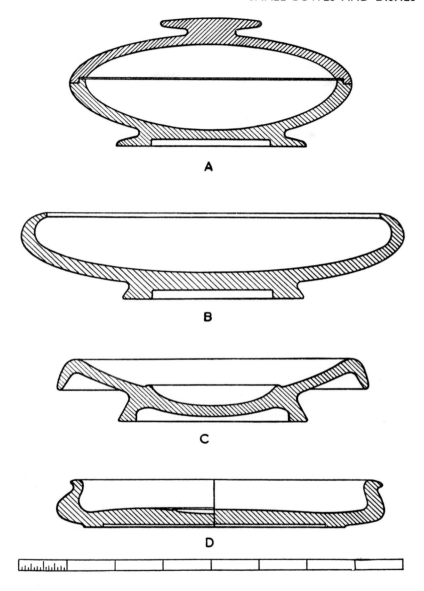

FIG. 5. SMALL BOWLS FOR SWEETS, NUTS, OR DRESSING TABLE ODDMENTS

6. BUILT-UP BOWLS

FIG. 1 SHOWS TWO designs (A and B) for a small bowl made up of six curved sections cut from a light-coloured hardwood. Between the sections is a thin strip of dark wood veneer which produces the pattern shown in the centre plan view (C). The method of assembly is similar to that used for the built-up clock cases, Fig. 3, page 49; but the cutting of the curved sections so that they fit accurately together presents a peculiar problem.

Curved sections. As it would be difficult to make these by hand a suitable wooden jig for use with a small band saw will be described later. The sections are cut from a 3 in. wide block which has been carefully planed to size. The depth of the block should be not less than $1\frac{3}{8}$ in. for the upper bowl (A) and $2\frac{3}{8}$ in. for the lower one (B), Fig. 1. The length required is about 15 in. which includes the waste piece left when the last section is cut off. In Fig. 2 the block is shown divided into sections by a series of saw-cuts on a $3\frac{1}{2}$ in. radius. There is, however, no need to mark these out if the jig is used, as this is designed to locate the work as each cut is made.

Jig. The construction of the jig is shown in Figs. 4 and 5. It will be seen that it consists of a flat base board provided with a vertical pivot on which the work carrier can rotate. The dimensions of the base must be made to suit the band saw table, and it should extend far enough to enable the jig to be firmly clamped in position. A $\frac{1}{4}$ in. wide slot is cut to clear the saw blade.

The work carrier has a vertical stop carefully positioned at one end and a curved slot through which the saw passes. The slot has a short length of straight to form a lead for the saw blade and facilitate lining up. The straight part of the slot should be carefully marked off and cut by hand with a relief on the inside edge to clear the saw blade when the work carrier swings outwards. The remaining curved portion is cut on the band saw after the jig is assembled and clamped in the correct position.

How jig works. The operation of the jig is shown in Fig. 6. The upper view shows the workpiece in position for the first cut, with the jig clamped to the band saw table so that the saw is just clear of the bottom of the slot in the base board, while at the same time locating centrally in the parallel portion of the slot in the work carrier. The band saw is then started and the carrier with its

66

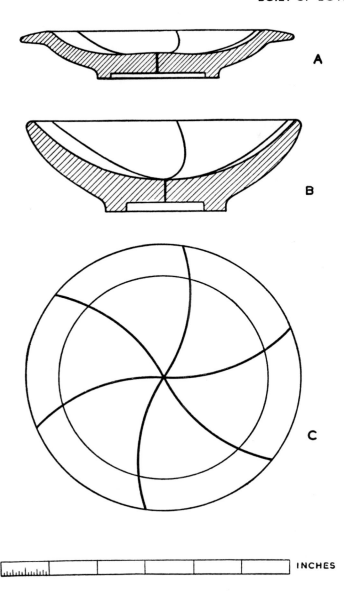

A

B

C

INCHES

FIG. I. BUILT-UP BOWLS MADE WITH CURVED SECTIONS

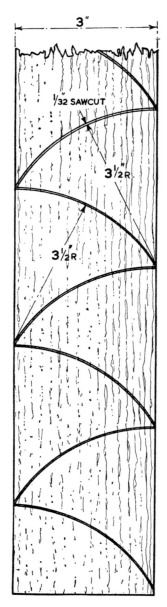

FIG. 2 (left). CURVED SECTIONS CUT FROM SINGLE PIECE

Jig for cutting is shown in Fig. 4

FIG. 3 (right). DETAIL OF CURVED SECTIONS SHOWING INLAY (A)

(B) shows the parts assembled ready for turning

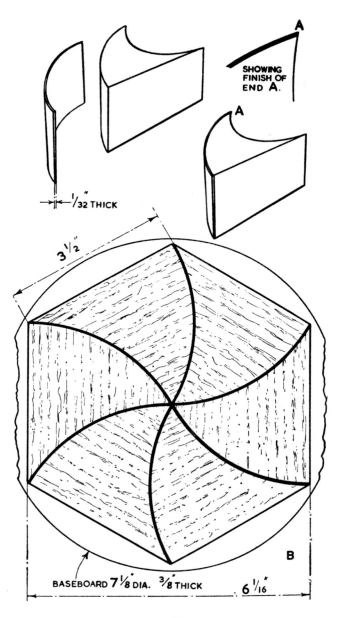

A

SHOWING
FINISH OF
END A.

A

$\frac{1}{32}$" THICK

$3\frac{1}{2}$"

B

BASEBOARD $7\frac{1}{8}$" DIA. $\frac{3}{8}$" THICK

$6\frac{1}{16}$"

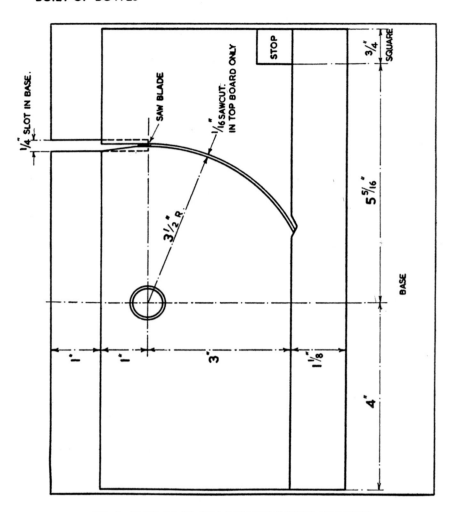

FIG. 4. PLAN OF JIG FOR CUTTING CURVED SECTIONS

workpiece swung through an arc to the position shown in dotted lines when the short waste piece will be cut off. The workpiece is next reversed, pushed up to the vertical stop and the process repeated, the first section then being completed. Successive reversals produce the remainder of the sections.

Assembling. Referring again to Fig. 3, one of the six sections is shown in the top view together with the thin strip of dark hardwood which is now glued on to the outside radius, the inner edge (A) being afterwards trimmed up as shown. The sections are now ready for assembly on a base board covered with paper and marked out as shown at (A), Fig. 7, the final assembly being shown at (B), Fig. 3. Reference should be made to methods described for building up the clock cases on page 52, as they apply equally well to this design. Special care, however, must be taken to see that all the lines meet at the correct point in the centre.

Turning. The methods adopted for turning the bowls are shown at (B and C), Fig. 7. Having carefully centred the work on the faceplate the top face is turned and the spigot recess bored. A waste block is next turned to fit and the work piece is attached by screws after the base board has been removed. The underside of the bowl can now be finished. Note that the recess in the bottom is made the same diameter as the original spigot so that the work can again be reversed for turning the inside without any alteration to the waste block.

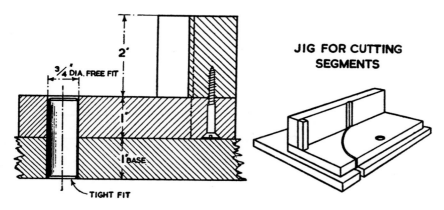

FIG. 5. SECTION THROUGH JIG; ALSO COMPLETED JIG

BUILT-UP BOWLS

FIG. 6 (below). JIG IN USE, SHOWING TWO STAGES

FIG. 7 (opposite). METHOD OF ASSEMBLING AND STAGES IN TURNING BOWL

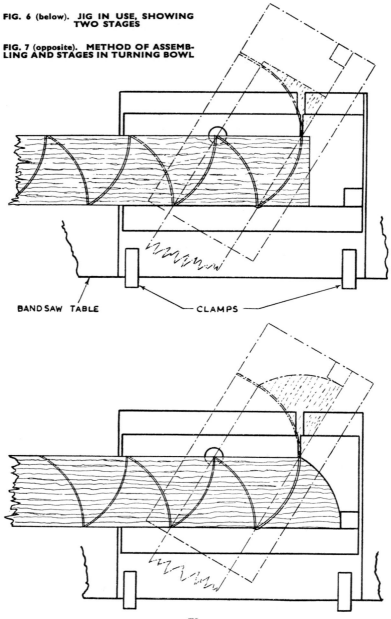

BAND SAW TABLE

CLAMPS

72

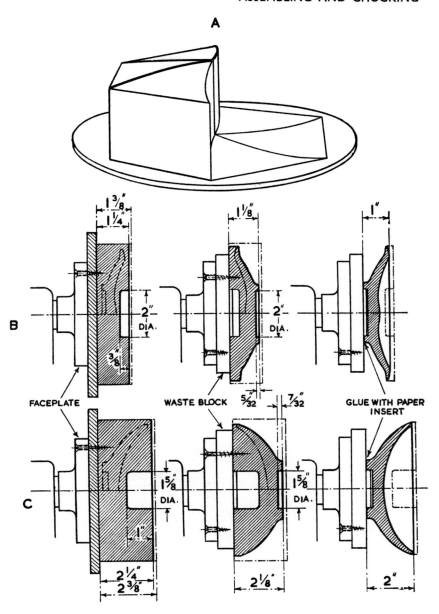

A

B

FACEPLATE

WASTE BLOCK

GLUE WITH PAPER
INSERT

C

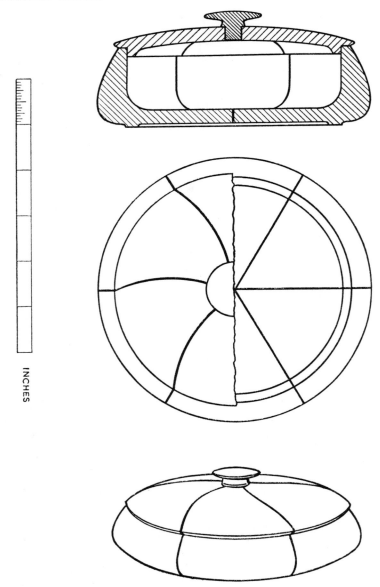

INCHES

FIG. 8. BUILT-UP BOWL WITH LID
Inlays can be straight or curved

74

BUILT-UP COVERED BOWL

As a further exercise in this kind of work the bowl in Fig. 8 has a lid made from six sections which can be cut on a jig similar to that already described. The bowl itself is built up from six segments in the same manner as the clock cases on page 50. As before $\frac{1}{32}$ in. thick strips of contrasting coloured wood are interposed between the vertical joints.

NOVEL SEGMENTAL BOWL

As an experiment the reader may be tempted to try his hand at one of the designs shown in Fig. 9. Here very accurate fitting of the six sectors which make up the bowl is essential. They should be trued up on their joint faces one at a time to match the lines marked out on the base board.

Turning the sectors. Six shallow cups are first turned as at (A), Fig. 10. Whichever contour is chosen, the six must be identical and to ensure this inside and outside templates should be prepared. The thickness at bottom and the over-all height must also be kept constant and the bottom surface turned flat to make good contact with the base to which it is later glued. The cups are next marked off and sawn to the shape shown at (B), Fig. 10, leaving a little material on each side for final truing. The edge is also reduced in height at the bottom of the V.

Assembling. The base board is next turned and marked out as shown at (C). Having glued and clamped the first sector in the position shown at (D), the second is carefully trued up until the contours match and the outer edge coincides with the next mark on the base. It will be noted that a space is left at the centre when the sectors are all fitted. This is covered by a rose glued in position after turning is completed.

The work is held in the lathe by gluing to a waste block as shown at (E).

LARGE SEGMENTAL BOWL

Fig. 11 shows a large fruit bowl made up of three rows of sectors cut from different coloured hardwoods to give a chequered effect. This method of building large-diameter rings is often resorted to in pattern making where it is important that the least amount of warping takes place. To achieve this object all the sectors must

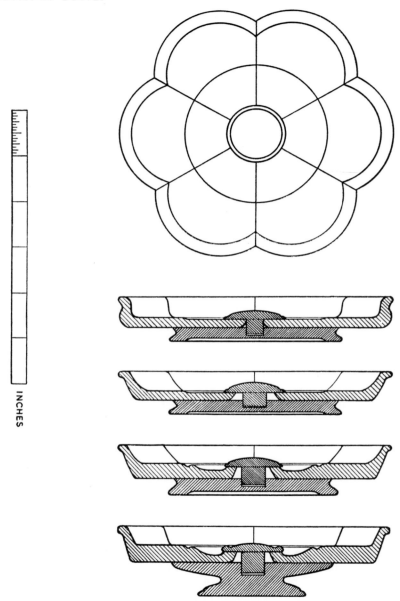

INCHES

FIG. 9. DESIGN IN WHICH SECTORS ARE TURNED AND CUT TO FIT

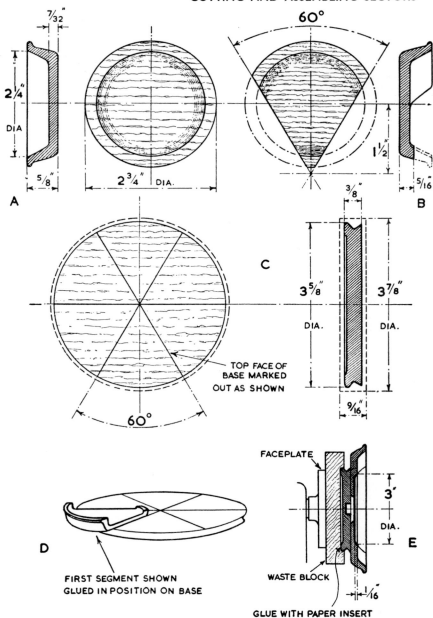

FIRST SEGMENT SHOWN
GLUED IN POSITION ON BASE

FACEPLATE

WASTE BLOCK

GLUE WITH PAPER INSERT

FIG. 10. SECTOR SIZES AND METHOD OF ASSEMBLING AND TURNING

BUILT-UP BOWLS

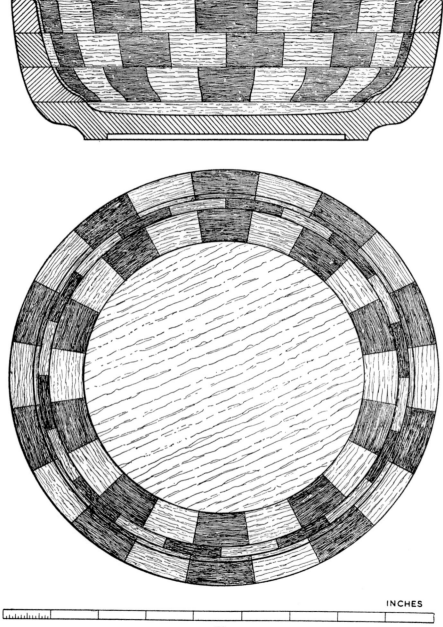

INCHES

be cut with the grain running lengthwise, the ring being then of uniform strength throughout. The usual method of laying out the sectors is shown at (A), Fig. 12, additional material being left on the inner and outer radii for subsequent turning. The sectors are cut out on the band saw and the ends carefully trued up to the correct angle so that they will fit together accurately and produce a good joint.

Sectors. Where the sectors are short as in the fruit bowl the sides can be left parallel and the pieces cut from material planed to size as shown at (B, C, and D), Fig. 12. There are twenty sectors in each row, the width varying in each. The depth should be $\frac{7}{8}$ in. in all cases to allow for facing the top of each row to a thickness of $\frac{3}{4}$ in. after assembly.

The base of the bowl is made in one piece and is first turned as shown at (E), Fig. 12, with a recess in the underside which will later be used for re-chucking. The top face is next marked out in 18 deg. divisions and the inside line of the bottom row marked as shown at (B) on the right-hand side so that the sectors can be accurately positioned.

Assembling. As each sector is glued it must be held with a separate clamp to the base so that twenty of these will be required. After the bottom row is completed, and the glue has set, the clamps are removed and the work is mounted on the faceplate for turning the top face of the sectors. This provides a flat surface for the second row, the joints of which occur midway between those of the bottom row. The work is fixed to a waste block during turning in the manner shown at (F), page 21. The screws fixing the work should be near the outer edge of the 5-in. spigot and their length carefully measured to make sure that they will not extend to the outside finished surface of the bowl. The joint lines and the inside line of the second row should now be marked and the second row glued and clamped as before. This is also faced before the top row is added and the work has reached the stage shown at (G), Fig. 12. The bowl is now ready for final turning, again locating from the recess to ensure concentricity.

As regards the choice of materials, four different-coloured hardwoods can be conveniently arranged in five sequences in each row. African walnut and sycamore combined with European walnut and beech is one suggestion to give an alternating light and dark pattern.

FIG. II (opposite). **BOWL BUILT-UP BRICK FASHION**
Really large bowls can be made using oddments of wood

BUILT-UP BOWLS

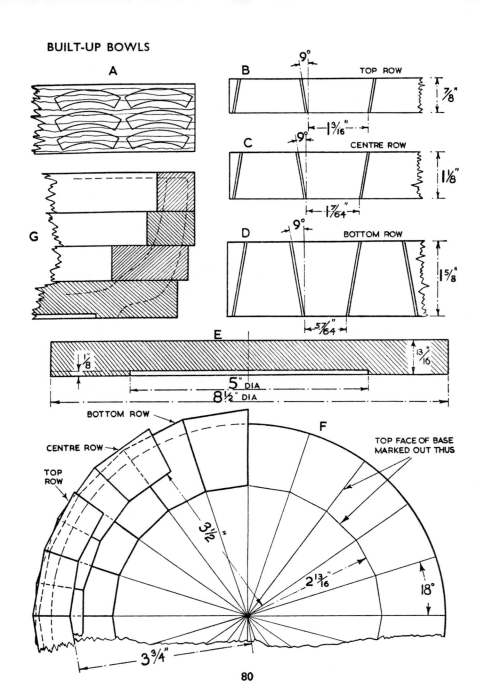

A

B **TOP ROW** 9° 7/8"

C **CENTRE ROW** 9° 1 3/16" 1 1/8"

D **BOTTOM ROW** 9° 1 7/64" 1 5/8" 5 7/64"

E 1/8" 13/16" 5" DIA 8 1/2" DIA

G

F
BOTTOM ROW
CENTRE ROW
TOP ROW
TOP FACE OF BASE MARKED OUT THUS
3 1/2"
2 13/16"
18°
3 3/4"

The base should preferably be turned from one of the lighter woods, sycamore being suitable for the purpose.

Finally, a word of warning is again given regarding glasspapering and polishing built-up work of this kind. Do not put too much pressure on the work otherwise the friction may generate sufficient heat to soften the glue.

BOWL WITH LID IN OAK AND SYCAMORE

FIG. 12 (opposite page). HOW "BRICKS" FOR BUILT-UP BOWL ARE PREPARED AND ASSEMBLED

7. VASES, JARS, AND BOXES

HARDWOOD VASES OFFER the turner plenty of scope for the exercise of his skill. Formerly "fruitwood" was in common use for small decorative work. Pear, apple, plum, and cherry were found to be admirable for the purpose on account of their excellent working qualities. Burr wood, more difficult to manipulate, was occasionally exploited for its unique grain markings. However, many of the examples in Figs. 1 and 2 will turn from one or other of the varieties of walnut. The two dice shakers (B), Fig. 1, and (E), Fig. 2, are exceptions as these were turned from boxwood.

TWO SIMPLE DESIGNS FOR VASES OR BEAKERS

They make effective spill holders. That to the right has gouge cut decoration at the bottom, but this could be omitted if preferred.

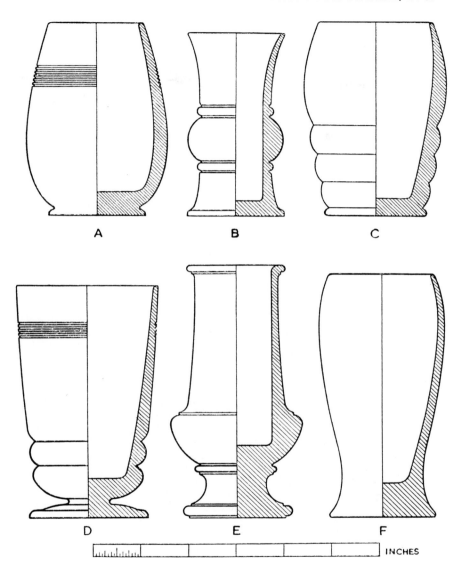

FIG. I. VASES, BEAKERS, DICE SHAKERS, ETC.

These are most interesting to turn and are excellent practice in hollowing out

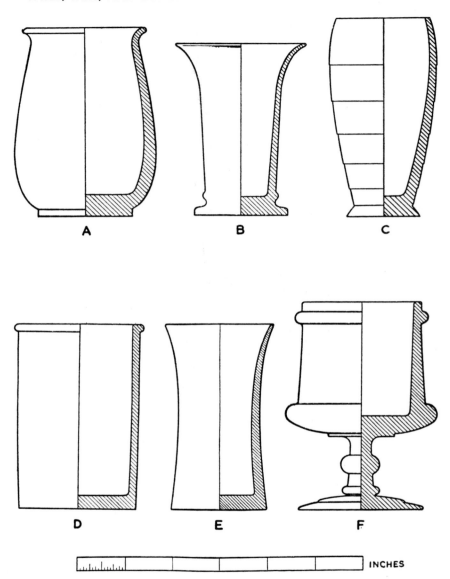

A B C

D E F

INCHES

FIG. 2. FURTHER DESIGNS FOR BEAKERS, ETC.

They should be turned in a close-grained hardwood

84

SPILL HOLDERS AND DICE SHAKERS

Chucking. In most cases the cup chuck will be found most convenient for holding the work as the outside shapes, finished mainly with scraping tools, can be turned without re-chucking. The hollowing of the inside presents some difficulty as the cutting edge of the tool eventually reaches a considerable distance from the tool rest and soon becomes unmanageable. To remedy this, a special side scraping tool as shown at (A), Fig. 3, should be obtained. This is used in conjunction with a hand rest held in the left hand and

USE OF EGG-CUP CHUCK FOR TURNING SMALL PART

A block of hardwood with centre hole is held in the chuck, and the wood to be turned hammered into the hole. The use of chalk helps the wood to grip

supported on the tool rest. The hand rest is bent up at right angles at the outer end to provide a bearing surface for the shank of the scraping tool.

In action the hand rest is pulled gently towards the operator and a light pressure is thereby applied to the cutting edge of the tool. Before commencing work with the side tool a parallel hole is first bored in the workpiece. This can be done with a machine twist-bit, preferably of the Jennings type, which has forward-projecting spurs.

85

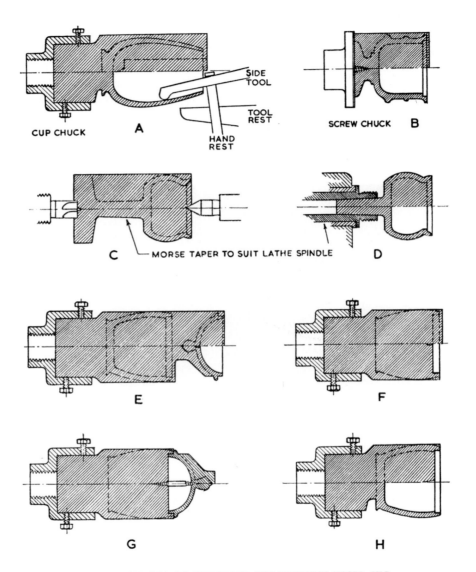

SIDE TOOL

TOOL REST

CUP CHUCK   A

HAND REST

SCREW CHUCK   B

C — MORSE TAPER TO SUIT LATHE SPINDLE

D

E

F

G

H

FIG. 3. METHODS OF CHUCKING AND TURNING VASES, ETC.

These enter the wood in advance of the main cutting edges and prevent the surface from splitting. The bit is fitted in the tailstock chuck and the lathe run at a very slow speed during this operation.

JARS AND BOXES

Fig. 4 shows a number of designs for covered ornamental jars and boxes. The large box, Fig. 5, is a copy of a string box once in common use, the string passing through the centre hole in the lid. It

SMALL DECORATIVE VASE

could equally serve as a tobacco jar or cigarette box. It could be made in sycamore when the appearance would be improved by applying a suitable grey stain before wax polishing. The small box (C), Fig. 4, is intended to be made from boxwood.

Turning. An alternative method of turning for the pedestal jar (F) is shown at (B), Fig. 3. Here the thickness of material in the base allows the screw chuck to be used, the base having been trued up and finished before the workpiece is screwed in position. A thin piece of waste wood is interposed between the face of the chuck and the workpiece so that the base can be turned without the tool coming into contact with the metal.

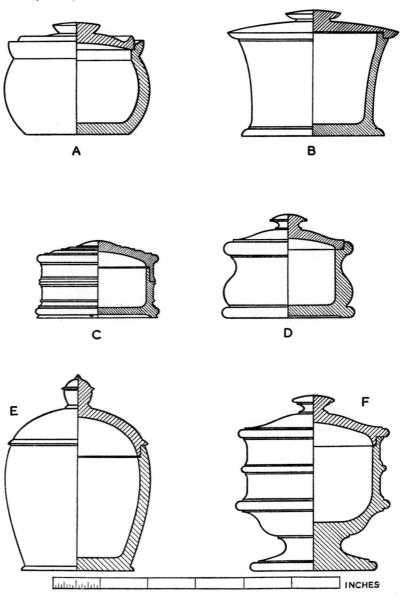

FIG. 4. TURNED BOXES WITH LIDS

Another method of turning sometimes adopted for small hollow articles is that shown at (C and D), Fig. 3. This shows the jar (A), Fig. 4, first turned externally between centres. A projection is left on the base which is cut to a Morse taper suitable for fitting directly into the lathe spindle. Naturally, the success of this method depends on a good fit being obtained and light cuts only can be made during the hollowing-out operations. Also care must be taken to see that enough space has been left between the end of the spindle and the bottom of the jar to allow the work to be parted off.

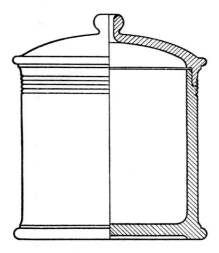

FIG. 5. TURNED STRING BOX

Turning jar and lid in one. Another method enabling the jar and the lid to be turned from the same workpiece is also shown in its various stages at (E, F, G, and H), Fig. 3. This relates to the jar (E), Fig. 4. The workpiece is mounted in the cup chuck and the end is turned to form the underside of the lid, which can be parted off after reaching the stage shown at (E). Note that a $\frac{3}{32}$ in. diameter centre hole about $\frac{3}{8}$ in. deep is first drilled with the aid of the tailstock chuck.

The workpiece is again faced, this time to form the top of the jar. The shallow recess turned in the end at (F) must engage snugly with the spigot already turned on the lid. Again a $\frac{3}{32}$ in. diameter centre hole is drilled with the tailstock chuck to a depth of about $\frac{1}{2}$ in. The lid can now be re-chucked on the workpiece as shown at (G) and it is held in position by a dowel screw which is first driven home

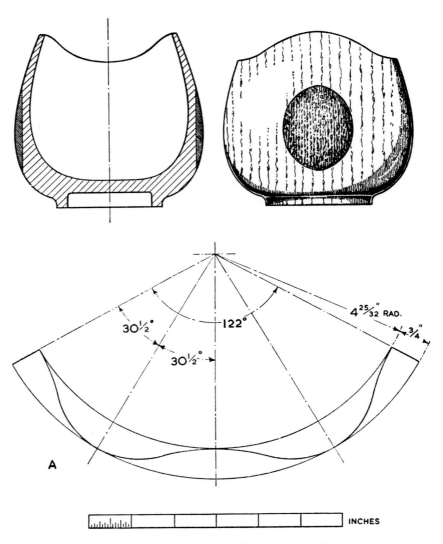

FIG. 6. CONTAINER WITH SHAPED EDGES AND APPLIED PLAQUES

in the workpiece. The screw should be checked for run-out before the lid is screwed in position. The outside shape of the lid can then be finish-turned and polished.

It will, of course, be necessary to plug the screw hole in the underside of the lid after removal from the lathe. For the example given the size of the dowel screw was 2 in. long, No. 10.

SUGAR SIFTER IN HARDWOOD

The method of chucking and hollowing out is similar to that of the other vases, beakers, etc. given in this chapter. The sifter at the top is a separate turning. It passes down about I in. into the container. Saw cuts down the sides enable it to give yet be a tight fit.

For screwing into the workpiece it is held on the parallel portion with pliers while the lathe is rotated by hand. It now remains to complete the turning of the jar, which can be glasspapered and polished before final parting off at the base, as at (H), Fig. 3.

LARGER DECORATIVE VASE

The design shown in Fig. 6 has two plaques which are produced by gluing two small blocks of a different-coloured timber to the main workpiece before turning. Accurate centering of the work in the lathe is essential to ensure that the plaques are identical.

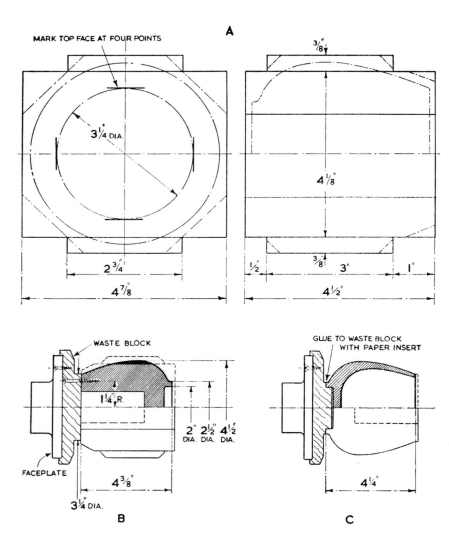

FIG. 7. CENTERING WOOD AND METHOD OF CHUCKING CONTAINER WITH APPLIED PLAQUES (see Fig. 6)

The workpiece is shown assembled at (A), Fig. 7 and, after being planed to size, is marked at four points so that it can be correctly positioned on the spigoted waste block shown at (B).

Some of the material can be removed from the inside by boring a hole down the centre by hand; but adequate room must be left for the wood screws which attach the workpiece to the waste block. The outside should be reduced by cutting off the corners at 45 deg. and rounding the remaining sharp edges. The ends of the two small blocks are also chamfered.

Chucking. Having mounted the work on the faceplate it is now checked for run-out from the outside faces of the two small blocks. Provided these have been made identical in thickness this check will ensure correct location and turning can be commenced. Re-chucking for finishing the inside is effected by turning the waste block down to form a spigot for the recess in the base of the vase and gluing the two together with a paper insert. The hollowing should be done entirely with scraper tools applied with light pressure.

Top shaping. The top of the vase will, of course, have to be cut carefully by hand, and for this purpose a paper template should be drawn to the dimensions shown at (A), Fig. 6. This is glued round the vase with the inside edge level with the top. The waste pieces can be cut away with either a fretsaw or a fine keyhole saw and the shape finished with glasspaper. The inside and outside edges should be finished with a small radius.

In choosing materials the main block for the vase should be the lighter colour. Avoid too great a contrast for the plaques—a black-and-white effect would be quite unsuitable. Sycamore and light walnut would be quite effective. On the other hand, a light walnut would combine with a darker variety or with coromandel.

Spherical bowl with lid. Begin by preparing the blocks for turning. That for the lid is about $3\frac{1}{4}$ in. square by $1\frac{3}{8}$ in. thick. For the bowl another piece of the same size is needed with a piece of sycamore $\frac{3}{4}$ in. thick glued to one side. To the other side a piece of waste wood about $\frac{7}{8}$ in. thick is glued. This is needed to provide a convenient attachment to the face plate, and to bring the work well away from the latter, so enabling the shape to be finished. The wood must be sound and dry because there will otherwise be trouble later owing to shrinkage and consequent warping.

Bowl. Fig. 12 shows how the bowl wood is mounted on the face plate. Screws can be driven directly through the latter into the waste block. Note that the square corners are sawn away so that excessive jolt is avoided when turning. Unless this is done the wood may easily split out.

The interior is hollowed out first, and, to enable the correct shape to be followed, a template should be made in thin card as in Fig. 11 (A). Note the projecting side pieces which enable the exact depth to be tested. It is necessary to use a rounded scraping tool to finish off.

For the outside a second template is needed, and it can be as shown in Fig. 11 (B). Begin by rough turning the whole to cylindrical shape, the diameter being a trifle more than the largest part of the bowl (this is over the small beads). Turn down the wood

FIG. 8. SPHERICAL BOWL WITH LID

leaving the beads projecting, and also the small square on which the bowl will stand. It is a help to remove a lot of the waste mounting block as this enables the tool to be used more easily on the rounded part of the bowl. This is shown in Fig. 10.

For finishing the tool must be really sharp and used with a light cut only. In this way all tears and other blemishes can be taken out. The beads need careful finishing, and only light cuts should be taken. The simplest way is to use a narrow, straight tool, and

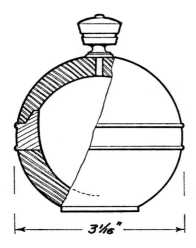

FIG. 9. SIZE AND SHAPE OF BOWL

3¹⁄₁₆"

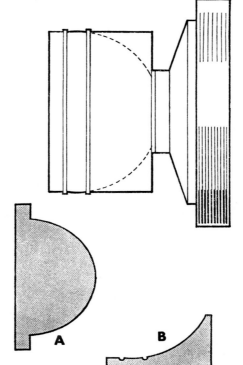

FIG. 10. HOW BOWL IS CHUCKED

FIG. 11. TEMPLATES FOR TURNING
A. Interior   B. Exterior

A

B

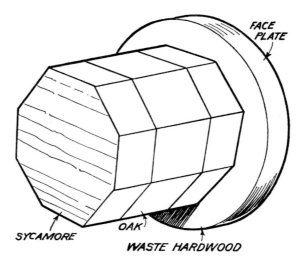

FACE PLATE

SYCAMORE   OAK   WASTE HARDWOOD

FIG. 12. BUILT-UP WOOD ON FACEPLATE

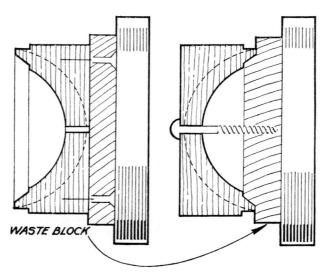

WASTE BLOCK

FIG. 13. TURNING LID ON WASTE BLOCK

sweep it round so that little curves are formed. The sloping rebate at the top completes the tool work, leaving only the final cleaning with glasspaper.

Before severing the bowl from the waste block it should be polished —either wax or lathe french polish.

Lid. Two chuckings are required. The inside is turned first, the wood being fixed to a waste block with screws as in Fig. 13. Note that the screws are driven in near the edges so that they enter a part of the wood which is removed later. Hollow the interior, using a template as for the bowl, and also turn the outside to slightly over the finished size. At the middle drill a hole right through to take the dowel which will hold the knob. It will probably be found easier to drill this before turning the inside, and will simplify the latter in that there will be no centre pip. Before removing from the waste block the inside can be polished.

To enable the wood to be centred exactly the waste block should have a spigot turned on it over which the inside of the bowl will fit exactly. Fix it with a screw through the centre hole as in Fig. 13 and it will be found to run quite true. Turn down the outside, using a template as before, and form the rebate so that it makes a close fit with the bowl. Finally polish.

The wood for the knob can be held in any convenient way—in the cup chuck, bell chuck, self-centreing chuck, or between centres.

SMALL PLATTER FOR SWEETS, ETC.

The small plastic container is the transparent lid used with many of the wrapped cheese cartons

97

8. BISCUIT BARRELS OR CASKETS, AND PLINTHS

THE FIRST CONSIDERATION in making a biscuit barrel is the size of the white china or earthenware liner and the source of supply of this necessary fitting. The usual dimensions are $4\frac{7}{16}$ in. maximum outside diameter and $4\frac{7}{16}$ in. over-all height. However, the liner should be obtained beforehand.

FIG. I. BISCUIT BARREL WITH LINER

Dark wood is sandwiched between the staves

FIG. 2 (opposite page). SECTIONAL ELEVATION AND PLAN

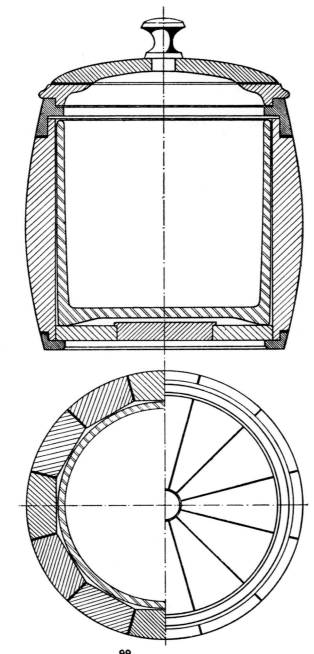

INCHES

99

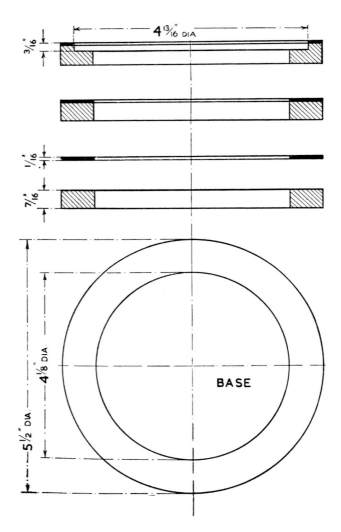

FIG. 3. SIZES OF RINGS FOR BASE OF BARREL

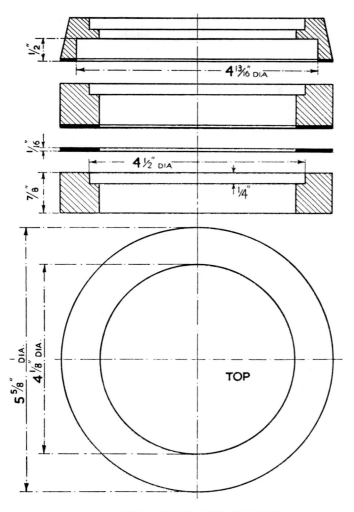

FIG. 4.   DETAILS OF TOP RING OF BARREL

BUILT-UP BISCUIT BARREL

The biscuit barrel in Fig. 1 is designed to fit this size container and it is shown in the sectional view in Fig. 2. Both the body of the barrel and the cover are built up of twelve sectors cut from light-coloured hardwood separated by thin strips of a darker material to produce the lines shown in Fig. 1. Though many biscuit barrels are provided with plated metal fittings this is made entirely from wood. The methods described for building up and turning the work can also be applied to the more conventional design where the sectors are glued together without the veneer insertions, in which case the barrel could be divided into a smaller number of sectors and the cover made in one piece.

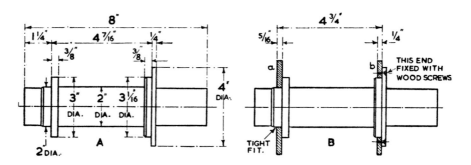

FIG. 5. MANDREL TO HOLD WOOD WHEN TURNING BARREL

Top and bottom. Figs. 3 and 4 give the dimensions for turning the rings which form the top and bottom of the barrel. These are turned on the faceplate; and a $\frac{1}{16}$ in. thick lamination of the darker wood is glued to the underside of the top ring and to the top of the base as shown.

Built-up body. We now come to the more difficult job of building up the body of the barrel. For this the mandrel shown at (A), Fig. 5 is first turned between centres. Two discs are prepared to the dimensions given in Fig. 6 (a and b). The one with the smaller hole (a) is made from the same material as that used for the sectors as it forms the bottom of the barrel. If this is made a tight fit on the mandrel it will not be necessary to fix it in position with screws.

102

**FIG. 6. DISCS WITH FLATS
TO HOLD STAVES**

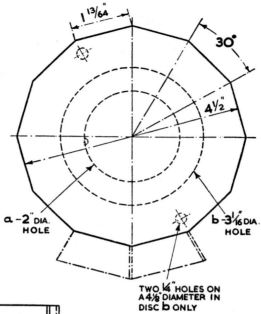

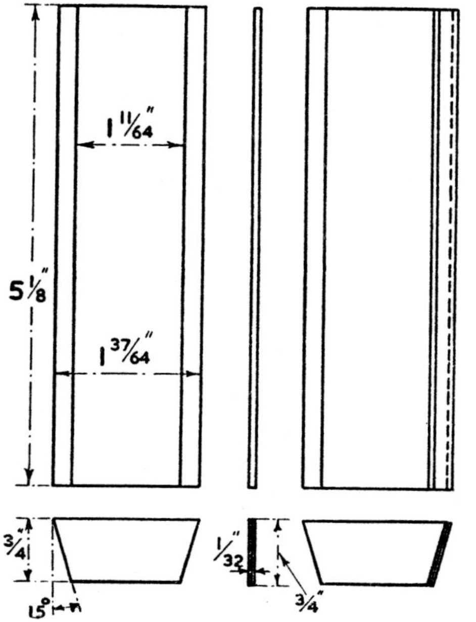

$1\frac{13}{64}''$

30°

$4\frac{1}{2}''$

5

a –2" DIA.
HOLE

b –3$\frac{1}{16}$ DIA.
HOLE

TWO ¼" HOLES ON
A 4⅛" DIAMETER IN
DISC **b** ONLY

$5\frac{1}{8}''$

$1\frac{11}{64}''$

$1\frac{37}{64}''$

$\frac{3}{4}''$

$\frac{1}{32}''$

15°

$\frac{3}{4}''$

**FIG. 7. DETAIL OF STAVES OR
SECTORS**

103

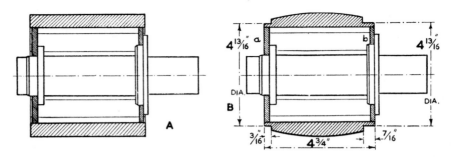

FIG. 8. PARTS MOUNTED ON MANDREL FOR TURNING

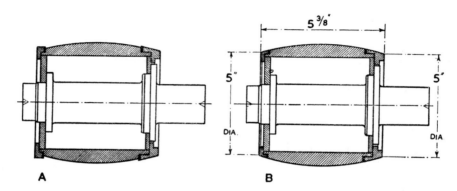

FIG. 9. LATER STAGES IN TURNING ON MANDREL

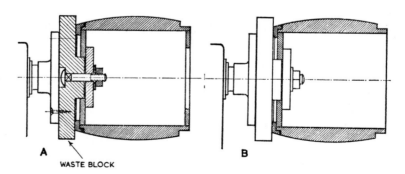

FIG. 10. WORK ON WASTE PIECE WITH SPIGOT FIXED TO FACEPLATE

The top disc (*b*) which can be made from any convenient waste wood, however, is fixed to the mandrel flange with wood screws. The flats on the outside of the discs must be accurately spaced and the sizes carefully maintained on both. Also, when mounted on the mandrel the discs must be positioned so that the flats are exactly in line.

The dimensions of the sectors are shown in Fig. 7 together with the lamination which is glued to one side. In assembling, the sectors are glued to the flats on both discs as well as to their adjacent joint faces, the complete assembly being shown at (A), Fig. 8. After the glue has set the outside of the barrel can be turned between centres to the sizes given at (B).

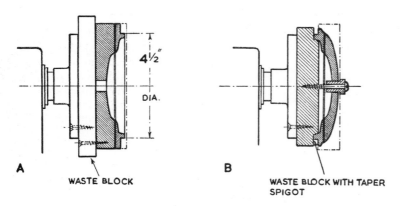

A WASTE BLOCK

B WASTE BLOCK WITH TAPER SPIGOT

FIG. 11. STAGES IN TURNING LID OF BISCUIT BARREL

Adding top and bottom. The top and bottom rings are now fitted, the base being permanently glued in position. As the top ring has to be removed and therefore cannot be glued, it must be made a tight fit on the spigot to allow the outside to be turned to match the shape of the barrel. This operation is shown at (A and B), Fig. 9.

The work is now removed from the lathe and the mandrel withdrawn after taking out the screws holding it to the top disc. The top ring can be removed by passing a $\frac{3}{16}$ in. diameter rod through the hole in the base and through the small holes drilled near the edge of the top disc, until it contacts the underside of the ring. When the ring has been moved a little on one side by gently tapping with a hammer, place the rod in the hole on the opposite side and tap that off a little. The process is then repeated until the ring is free.

A waste block similar to that shown at (A) and (B), Fig. 10 is now required so that the barrel can be re-chucked for turning out the top ring. It is spigoted on the 2 in. diameter hole in the base and is held in position by a coach bolt. The ring is turned away until the tool reaches the flats on the sectors, when a hole $4\frac{1}{2}$ in. diameter is produced for the depth of the ring. The remainder of the barrel bore need not be turned as it is out of sight when the liner is fitted.

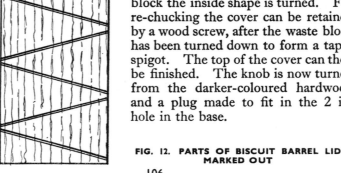

Cover. The construction of the cover is shown in Figs. 12 and 13. The sectors are first cut to the dimensions shown in Fig. 12, after which the thin laminations are glued to one side. A base board (A), Fig. 13 forming the lower half of the lid is next prepared and a $\frac{1}{16}$ in. lamination (B) is glued to one face. The laminations are, of course, again made from the same material as those for the barrel. The sectors are glued to the base board and the workpiece is ready for turning. A jig with a suitable work stop can be used for producing the sectors accurately. This is shown at (D). The suggested chucking arrangements for the cover are shown in Fig. 11 (A) and (B).

After centering the work on a waste block the inside shape is turned. For re-chucking the cover can be retained by a wood screw, after the waste block has been turned down to form a taper spigot. The top of the cover can then be finished. The knob is now turned from the darker-coloured hardwood and a plug made to fit in the 2 in. hole in the base.

FIG. 12. PARTS OF BISCUIT BARREL LID MARKED OUT

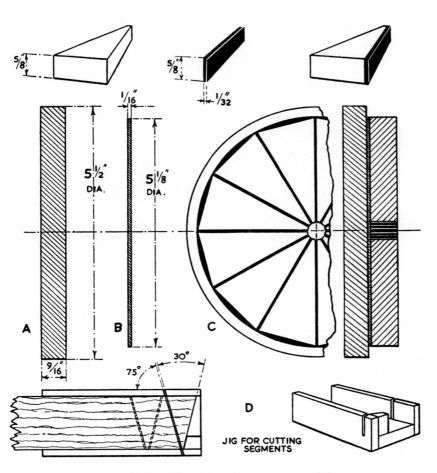

5/8"

5/8"

1/32"

1/16"

5½" DIA.

5⅛" DIA.

A

B

C

9/16"

75°

30°

D

JIG FOR CUTTING SEGMENTS

FIG. 13. DETAIL OF THE LID SEGMENTS, AND HOW THEY ARE CUT OUT AND ASSEMBLED. ALSO JIG FOR CUTTING

If the liner is found to be a little loose in the barrel it should be packed with paper on the outside diameter until it is tight, after which the top ring can be fitted in position.

Photograph by courtesy of the Coronet Tool Co. Ltd.

DEEP BORING ON THE LATHE

This is frequently needed for candlesticks etc. A special device for attachment to the lathe bed is available. This consists of a hollow ring centre of the same diameter as the normal centre. It is substituted, and the special boring tool is passed in from the end as shown.

SMALL BARREL

The design in Fig. 14 makes use of a 1 lb. marmalade jar as a liner. This is the white earthenware type. The body of the barrel is made up of six segments which are again assembled on a mandrel for turning as shown on the accompanying sketches. Oak or walnut is suggested for the barrel and cover. It can be finished either by wax or french-polishing as desired.

The method of building-up and turning is similar to that of the biscuit barrel on page 98. Two hexagonal pieces are needed, one with a 2 in. centre hole, and one with a 1½ in. hole. Sizes are given in Fig. 15. It is convenient to turn the wood for the hexagons, and work the flats afterwards. These are mounted upon the special

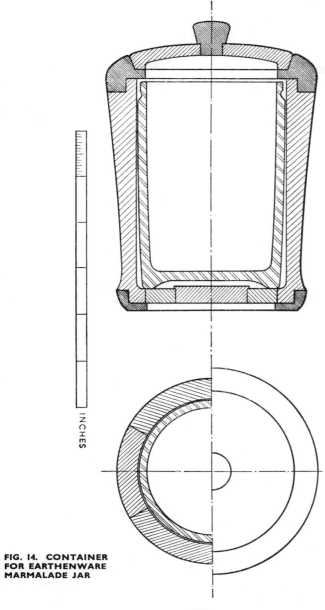

INCHES

FIG. 14. CONTAINER
FOR EARTHENWARE
MARMALADE JAR

mandrel shown in Fig. 15. To these hexagons are fixed the staves which form the cylindrical shape. A section through these staves is given in Fig. 16, and exact planing of the sides to give an included angle of 60 deg. is important. A good plan is to fix a block of wood

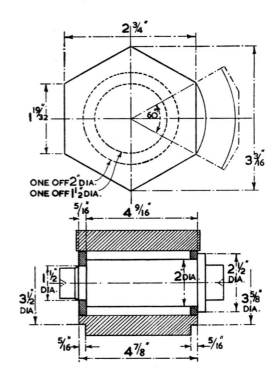

FIG. 15. MANDREL AND HEXAGONS USED FOR TURNING BODY OF MARMALADE JAR

to the shooting board, this being tapered so that the plane automatically works at the required angle. It helps the turning if the outer corners are taken off, but it is not essential. The most awkward stave is the last one, and the best way is to make the width slightly full and skim the edge until it just drops in comfortably, the sides making a close fit, and the underside bedding upon the hexagons. If by mischance too much is taken off the sides, a shaving from the underside will put things right.

Rebates are cut at top and bottom to take the rings, details of which are given in Fig. 16.

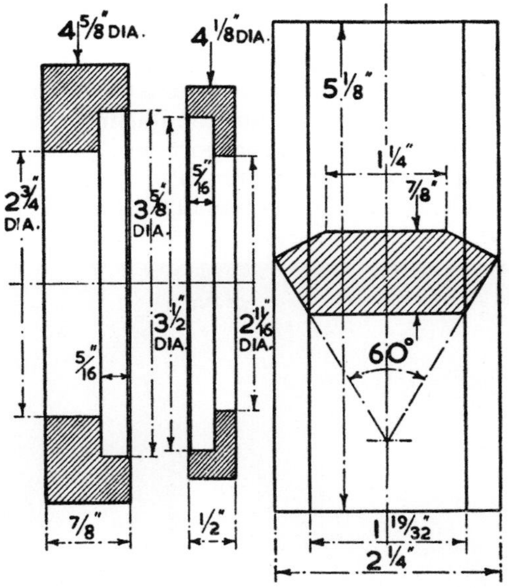

FIG. 16. DETAILS OF TOP AND BOTTOM RINGS AND STAVES OF MARMALADE JAR

TURNED PLINTHS

Plinths for mounting silver cups, china or metal vases, and small pieces of statuary are nearly always turned in classical style somewhat resembling the bases of architectural columns. For bronze statuary the plinth is often drilled to accommodate a central stud screwed into the base of the statue. The piece can be secured by a nut fitting into a recess in the underside of the plinth. Fig. 17 shows a selection, all of which are intended to have a matt black finish resembling ebony.

Although genuine ebony may occasionally be used for small work the cost of this timber prohibits its general use. It is, therefore, common practice to turn plinths from other hardwoods and

111

apply a dense black stain, the part then being polished to a high finish. The matt surface is obtained by rubbing down with a super-fine abrasive pumice powder. The stains and abrasive powders for this process (which is known as ebonising) are readily obtainable from dealers and are made up to suit various types of wood. The darker varieties of walnut are especially suitable for high-class work. On the other hand a satisfactory result can be obtained by using a soft wood such as American whitewood, for example, which is easily worked and takes the stain well.

Obviously no specific dimensions can be laid down for these articles as they must be made to measure, but the illustrations will serve as a general guide to outlines and proportions. The large centre plinth (C) is copied from a pair of French bronzes. The top has a shallow spigot which registers in a recess in the base of the bronze.

MODERN TURNINGS WITH SIMPLE, CLEAN LINES

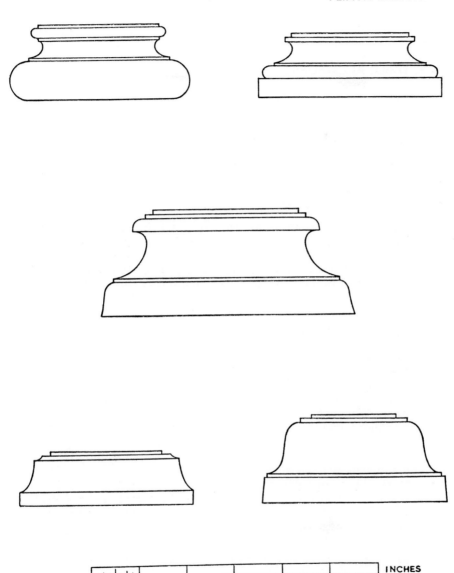

INCHES

FIG. 17. PLINTHS OR PEDESTALS FOR PRESENTATION CUPS, TROPHIES, ETC.

113

9. TABLE ACCESSORIES

BEFORE THE GENERAL introduction of pottery in the 18th century our forefathers made wide use of turned wooden tableware, and much skill was displayed by the turners in the production of drinking vessels, plates, and bowls. Nowadays the use of wood is restricted to such small accessories as condiment sets, teapot stands, serviette rings, egg cups, etc.

AN EGG-CUP STAND

Fig. 1 shows a design for an egg-cup stand turned from Japanese oak and finished with wax polish. Alternative designs are given for the handle at (A) and (B) with feet to match. The base is turned on the faceplate and the various designs of egg cup can be turned on the screw chuck or in the cup chuck, scraping tools being used for most of the work.

SERVIETTE RINGS

The small articles shown in Fig. 2 afford opportunities for using up odd pieces of hardwood left over as waste from previous larger work. The serviette rings shown at (A) are good examples. Various methods can be devised for turning thin rings of this description. One way is to turn them with the block mounted on the screw chuck when they can be finished inside and out before parting off.

An easier method is to bore the block first with a slightly tapered hole and mount it on a taper mandrel previously turned between centres. The slow taper will enable the block to be fitted tightly on the mandrel when the outer diameter can be turned and polished. Close-grained wood should preferably be chosen for such thin sections and the finish must be first class.

TABLE MATS FOR DRINKING GLASSES

These tiny articles, (B), Fig. 2, can also be made from odd pieces of close-grained wood finished either by french polishing or clear cellulose varnish which will give better protection for the wood.

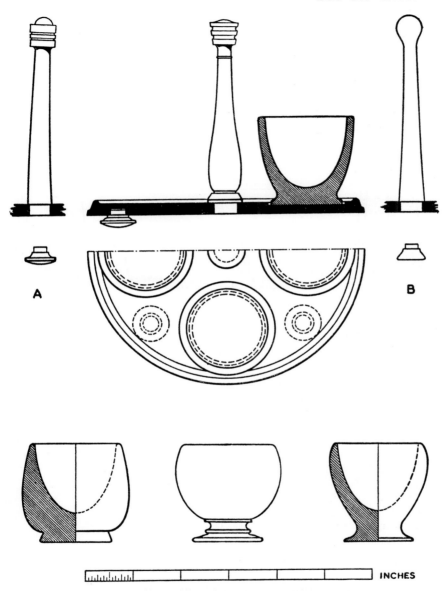

FIG. I. EGG CUP CRUET WITH ALTERNATIVE CUP DESIGNS

INCHES

115

TABLE ACCESSORIES

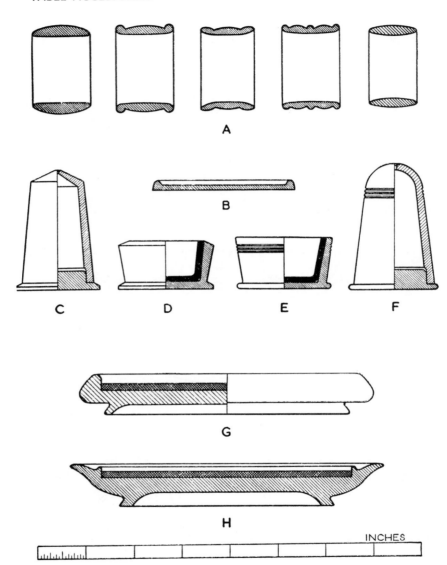

FIG. 2. SERVIETTE RINGS, CONDIMENT CONTAINERS, AND TEA POT STANDS

116

CONDIMENT SETS

Two alternative styles are shown at (C) and (D), and at (E) and (F). They can be produced from oak or walnut and should be given a wax-polished finish. The pepper and salt containers are identical except for the holes in the top and the mustard pots will have to be bored to suit the small glass containers. These articles can all be turned in the cup chuck and care must be taken to make the base of the pepper and salt containers a tight fit to the body.

PEPPER MILL

This (below) incorporates the special metal fitting shown in fig. 13. The collar is fitted into the base of the mill and retained by the cross bar. The grinder itself passes upwards before the cross bar is fitted, and its square shaft emerges through a hole in the lid, the latter being secured by the top nut. A disc having a square centre hole screwed beneath the lid forces the grinder to turn as the lid is revolved. Some adjustment in height is usually needed. The sectional view shows the shape to which the mill and lid are turned. Note the shallow step to enable the collar to be accommodated.

There are two ways of turning the shape. The first is to turn the wood between centres to the fullest part but with the top end made to a close fit in the cup chuck. There should be enough extra in length to fit in this. There should also be about $\frac{1}{2}$ in. extra in length at what will be the bottom end. Fit the wood into the cup chuck and part bore and part turn the centre hole including the bottom two steps. Light cuts are necessary to avoid forcing the wood out of truth. The outside is also turned and finally parted off near the cup chuck. The wood is now reversed and fitted into a recess turned in a waste piece attached to the face plate, and the small rebate at the top turned. When all is satisfactory the whole thing is parted off at the base.

PEPPER MILL IN LIGNUM VITAE

TABLE ACCESSORIES

In the second method the wood is turned between centres, then fixed top end in the cup chuck with a waste piece at the bottom. Again there is ample left for parting off later. The centre is bored out including the two bottom steps, light cuts only being taken. A mandrel is turned between centres to make a close fit for the inside of the mill. A *slight* taper helps. The outer shape is now turned, and the small step at the top completed.

To turn the lid fix the wood to a waste piece with glue, using paper in the joint to enable it to be removed later. Screw the waste piece to the face plate, and turn the inside of the lid including the groove. Also the sides and the centre hole. Reverse the wood into a hole turned in a waste piece. It should make a tight fit, but is additionally held with a screw passed through the centre hole. The top can now be turned.

FIG. 3. PEPPER MILL

Below is sectional view and details of the metal fitting

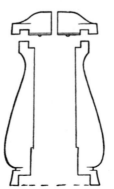

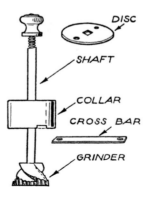

DISC

SHAFT

COLLAR

CROSS BAR

GRINDER

118

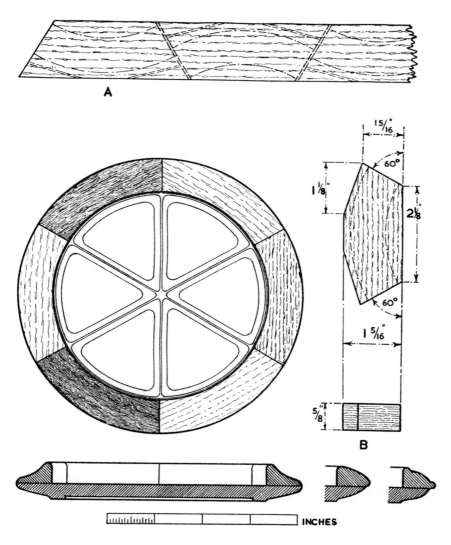

FIG. 4. DISH TO HOLD WRAPPED CHEESE PORTIONS

TEAPOT STANDS

The two teapot stands (G and H), Fig. 2 are turned on the face-plate. Oak is suggested. The stands have a recess in the top face into which a cork mat is fitted.

BUILT-UP CHEESE DISH

This is designed to hold one of the circular cardboard boxes in which the popular wrapped cheese portions are sold. As there are six portions in each packet the dish is built up of six sectors to

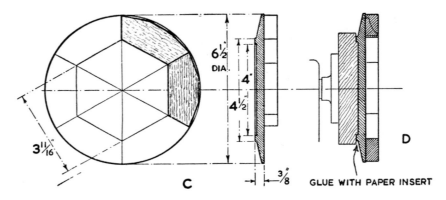

FIG. 5. ASSEMBLING CHEESE DISH AND METHOD OF CHUCKING

match as shown in Fig. 4. These can all be different in colour preferably with light and dark alternations. The inside diameter of the finished dish should be a little over $4\frac{1}{2}$ in. If a number of dishes are to be made, six lengths of different wood can be cut into the shapes shown at (A). The dimensions of the individual sector are shown at (B).

The base board made from dark timber is turned up on the faceplate and the top face marked out as shown at (C), Fig. 5, the sectors then being glued in position and clamped. A waste block (D), is prepared with a spigot to fit the shallow recess in the bottom face. It is necessary to glue the dish in position with a paper insert in order to turn the inside and form the outer edge. Further suggestions

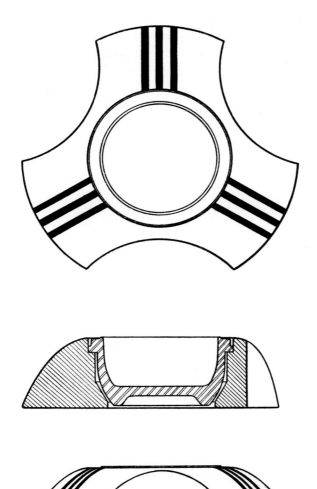

FIG. 6. BUILT-UP ASH TRAY WITH DARK INLAY LINES

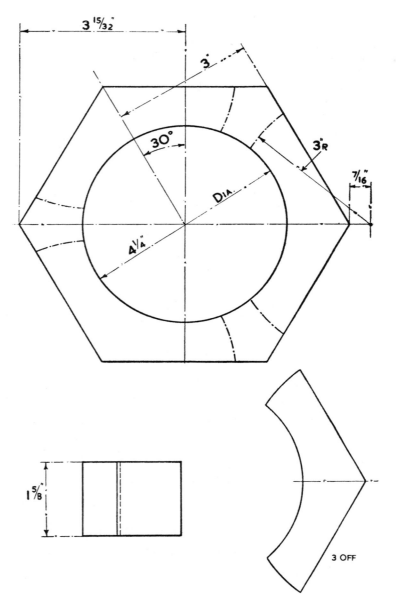

FIG. 7. HEXAGONAL BLOCK FROM WHICH PARTS ARE CUT

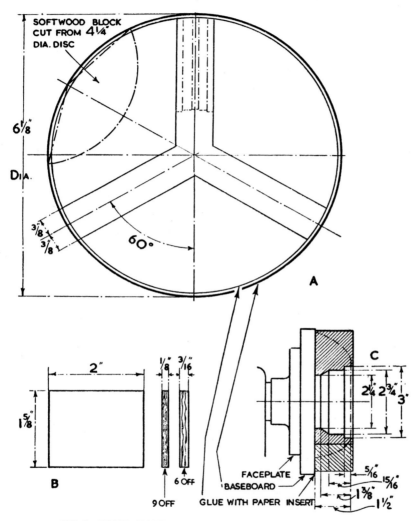

SOFTWOOD BLOCK
CUT FROM 4¼"
DIA. DISC

6⅛"

DIA.

⅜"
⅜"

60°

A

2"

1⅝"

⅛" 3/16"

B

9 OFF

6 OFF

FACEPLATE
BASEBOARD
GLUE WITH PAPER INSERT

C

2¼" 2¾" 3"

5/16"
15/16"
1⅜"
1½"

FIG. 8. PARTS GLUED TO BASE WITH INTERVENING PAPER

The inlays are shown at (B), and method of fixing to faceplate for turning
internal shape.

123

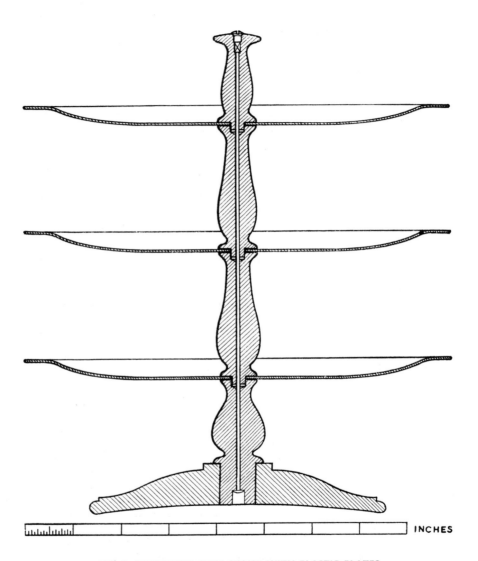

INCHES

FIG. 9. THREE-TIER CAKE STAND WITH PLASTIC PLATES

for the rim treatment are also given. Almost any hardwoods may be used for the sectors, one suggested combination being arranged in this order—American walnut, maple, mahogany, sycamore, haldu, beech, or light oak.

BUILT-UP ASH TRAY

This is intended as an experiment. As seen in Fig. 6 it is built round the white opaque glass jar which originally contained a popular brand of fish paste.

It is cut from the hexagonal-shaped block shown at (A), Fig. 7. The three sections are glued to the marked-out baseboard (A), Fig. 8 which has previously been covered with paper. Between the sections are glued the laminations of contrasting coloured wood shown at (B), 9 off, together with six thicker laminations of the same lighter-coloured wood from which the main sections have been cut.

Faceplate turning. Before mounting the base board on the faceplate for final turning, three softwood blocks should be glued to the base only in the position shown in (A) to fill the gaps temporarily so preventing an interrupted cut. In this way the outside shape will be left with a clean, sharp edge. Sycamore and walnut already suggested for previous built-up work could again be used. The bore should be made so that the glass container seats on the top shoulder, the outside diameter of which is a tight fit in the wood. Any other suitable container can be used and the bore modified accordingly.

THREE-TIER CAKE STAND

Although the design in Fig. 9 may have little commercial value it is simple to construct and forms a useful accessory for the tea table. The five sections can be turned from oak or walnut, the lower section and the base only being glued together. The remainder of the sections spigot into one another. The whole assembly is held together by a cycle spoke passing through a $\frac{3}{32}$ in. diameter hole drilled through the sections, the nipple fitting into a recess in the handle. This will be found to be amply strong enough to hold the stand rigid and will also allow it to be dismantled for cleaning. Transparent plastic plates can be used as these are easily drilled and their light weight is also an advantage in this design.

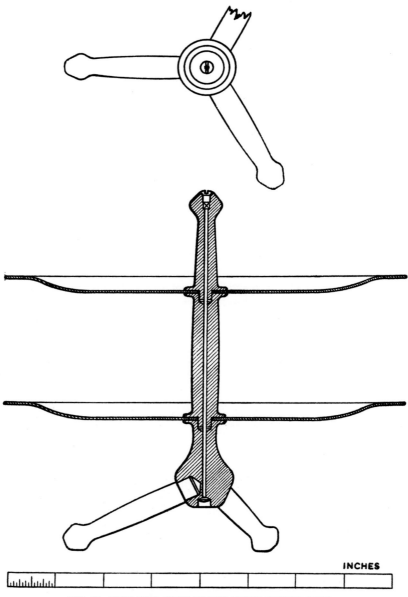

FIG. 10. TWO-TIER CAKE STAND WITH TRIPOD LEGS

INCHES

TWO-TIER CAKE STAND

Two more stands similarly constructed are shown in Figs. 10 and 11. Three legs glued into the lower section are provided in place of the circular base in the first example.

CAKE STAND WITH PLASTIC PLATES ON HARDWOOD STAND

This is similar to the design on page 124. The pillar consists of four separate spindles with spigot joints held together with a cycle spoke

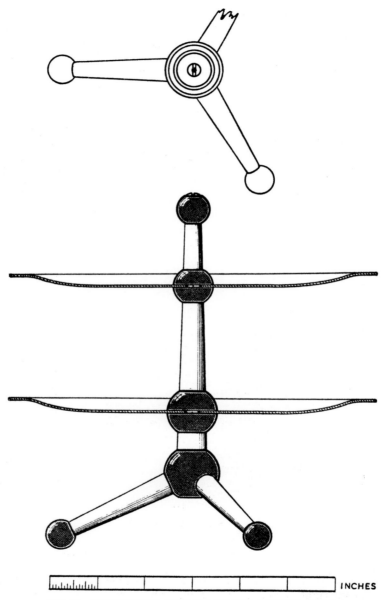

INCHES

FIG. 11. ALTERNATIVE CAKE STAND FOR PAINTED FINISH

Walnut or oak can be used for the design, Fig. 10; but the modern styled stand, Fig. 11, will look better with a two-colour finish, the ball shapes being dark and the stem light. In this case the balls could be turned separately from dark walnut stained black and spigoted to stems made from natural sycamore.

CRUET

The whole thing is turned in lignum vitae. The pepper mill has already been dealt with on page 117.

Salt cellar. For the salt cellar it is necessary to use two pieces as otherwise it is impossible to bore out the inside. The joint occurs immediately above the bottom hollow member as shown in

CRUET IN LIGNUM VITAE

Fig. 12. First fix the wood in either the cup chuck or the eggcup chuck, and bore the inside. Generally the wood is too hard for a large bit, and the usual plan is to start a small hole with a Morse drill. It will go right through and become the hole through which the salt emerges. Enlarge it with a bigger drill (not right through) and finally complete with a scraping tool. Note that the bottom of the hole (which becomes the top of the cellar) should be domed to a point. To enable the outside to be turned without risk of the wood starting out of truth a small disc with spigot and centre can be turned to fit the bottom of the cellar. Except for the preliminary roughing the outside can be turned with scraping tools.

The bottom can be mounted on a waste piece turned on the face-plate. A centre hole for a cork is needed, and the underside needs to be deeply recessed so that the cork does not project and prevent the cellar from standing upright.

LARGE VASE IN HARDWOOD

This measures 12 in. high by about 7 in. diam. and has thin walls. Such work calls for a heavily built lathe and firm anchorage on a face plate

Turned by S. W. Levine (Capetown)

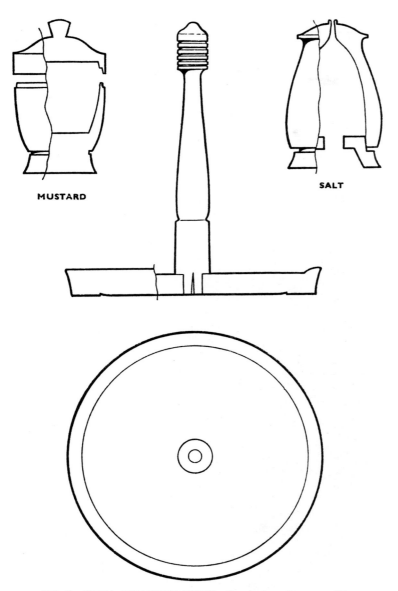

MUSTARD

SALT

FIG. 12. SMALL BREAKFAST CRUET. See photograph on page 129

Mustard pot. The simplest way of turning the pot is to allow about 2 in. extra length to enable the whole thing to be turned in the cup chuck. The mustard container is a plastic egg cup obtainable from Woolworths, cut down in height, and the inside of the pot should be hollowed to contain it. A small rebate around the top edge enables the lid to fit neatly. The wood is quite thin, and a dense hardwood such as lignum vitae is clearly desirable.

To turn the lid again use the cup chuck. Hollow the inside with its rebate, and turn the outside to align with the pot, the latter being offered up to it. As much of the top shaping as is practicable is also done, after which it is parted off, and reversed into a hollow cut in a waste piece. This enables the shaping and knob to be turned.

Stand. The base is a simple piece of faceplate turning. If a disc is glued to a waste piece with newspaper interposed, the whole thing including the centre hole can be turned in one operation. The stem is a simple piece of between-centre turning.

MODERN CONDIMENT SET IN HARDWOOD

Made by C. E. Bampton

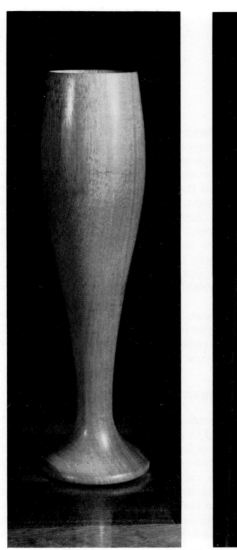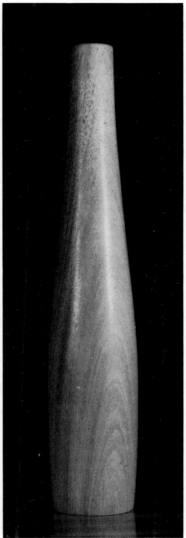

TALL VASE AND TABLE LAMP

These exemplify the value of simple, flowing shapes free from all fussy and
unnecessary detail.

10. WALL BRACKETS

SINGLE WALL BRACKETS

IN THE DESIGNS in Fig. 1 the platform to carry the plant pot has a taper stem which fits into the support bracket and can be turned from the solid with the workpiece held between centres. The support bracket will turn easily on the screw chuck. The taper hole must be put in by hand and the best way to do this is to start with a small pilot hole drilled right through which can be checked for position before proceeding further. Then, with the correct size bit for each end of the taper, a very shallow recess is put in both ends. The centre portion can then be removed by using smaller bits. A good fit need only be obtained for a short distance at each end as the parts are permanently glued together. If a taper reamer happens to be available the work will, of course, be simplified.

In both examples a small separate knob is glued into a hole in the base of the taper stem as a finish after the two main parts are assembled. The first design (A) calls for a polished hardwood finish. Oak or walnut stained as desired come first to mind.

SEMI-CIRCULAR FLOWER BOWLS

A further form of wall decoration is shown in Fig. 2. These articles must of course be turned in pairs and they can be produced by gluing two half blocks together for turning with a sheet of paper interposed, and fitting a thin plywood cover to the back after they have been separated. Another method is illustrated in Fig. 3. Here the half blocks are separated by a plywood lamination whose thickness is double that of the back board finally fitted to the bowl. The simplest way of achieving this is to glue two of the thin boards together. The lamination is glued to the blocks with a paper insertion on each side as shown at (A). The assembly is now screwed to the faceplate and the inside finished-turned with the slow taper shape given at (B), and the outside rough-turned. The two

FIG. I. SMALL TURNED BRACKETS FOR PLANTS AND ORNAMENTS

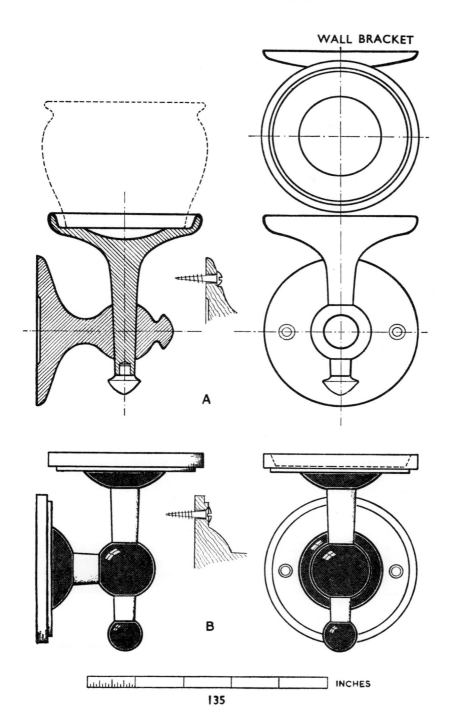

WALL BRACKET

A

B

INCHES

135

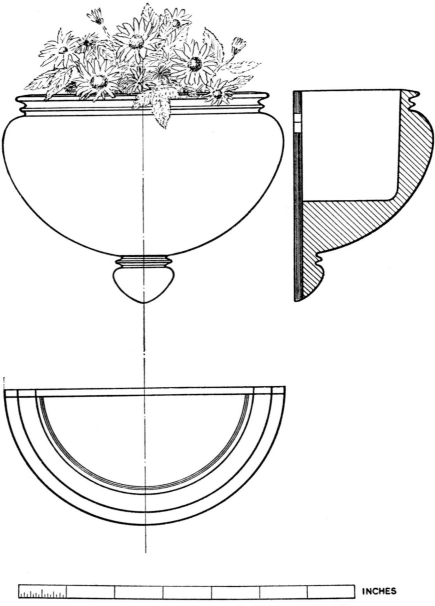

FIG. 2.   SEMI-CIRCULAR WALL VASE FOR FLOWERS, ETC.

INCHES

136

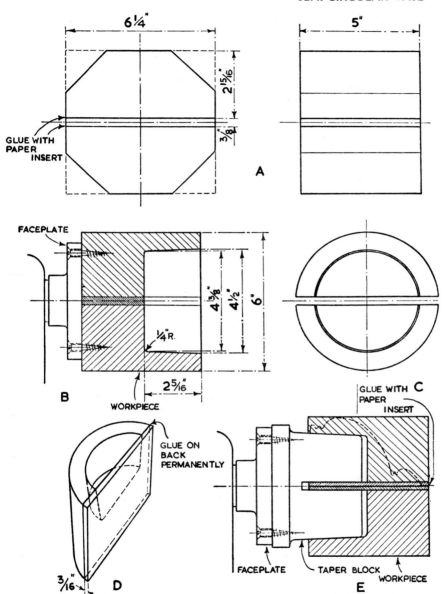

GLUE WITH
PAPER
INSERT

A

B

¼"R.

WORKPIECE

2⁵⁄₁₆"

FACEPLATE

4³⁄₈"
4½"
6"

GLUE WITH **C**
PAPER
INSERT

GLUE ON
BACK
PERMANENTLY

³⁄₁₆" **D**

FACEPLATE | TAPER BLOCK
WORKPIECE

E

6¼"

2¹⁵⁄₁₆"

³⁄₈"

5"

FIG. 3. HOW SEMI-CIRCULAR VASES ARE TURNED IN PAIRS

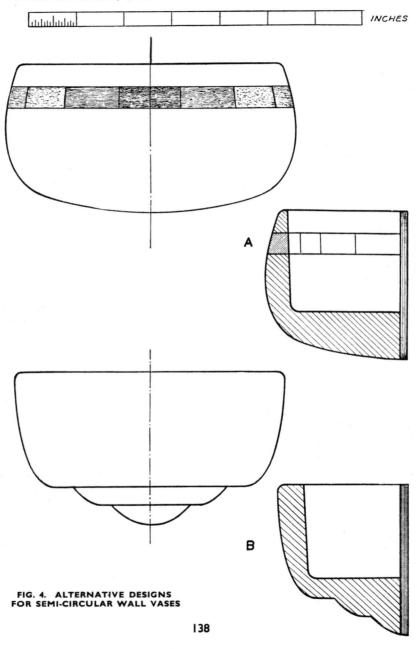

INCHES

A

B

FIG. 4. ALTERNATIVE DESIGNS
FOR SEMI-CIRCULAR WALL VASES

138

halves are separated and the final thin back board glued on each piece permanently.

Turning the outside. To turn the outside shape a taper waste block is first roughly turned up and a slot cut down the centre to accommodate the back boards. It is carefully brought down to size until the two halves fit snugly as shown at (E) with a sheet of paper between them. When a satisfactory fit has been obtained the paper can be glued, the two halves placed together and pushed on to the taper block so that they will line themselves up while the glue is still wet. The two halves are clamped together and left until the glue has set.

The work is replaced on the block and the outside turning completed. Obviously, heavy cuts must be avoided and as much material as possible removed by end facing so that the pressure of the tool tends to tighten the work on the taper. Scraping tools should be used for all finishing operations.

Alternative designs are shown in Fig. 4.

By courtesy of Coronet Tool Co. Ltd.

ECCENTRIC FIXING ON FACE PLATE FOR EGG CUP STAND

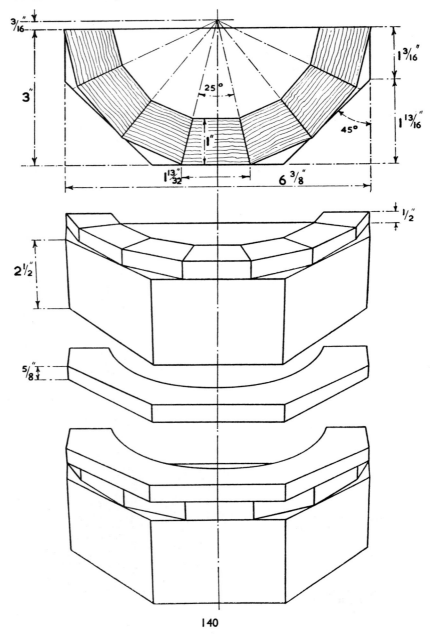

TWIST LAMP

This cannot be finished in its entirety on the lathe as a turning operation, but obviously the main basic shape is turned. The centre hole for the flex is bored first, the hollow back-centre being

**TURNED AND CARVED
TWIST TABLE LAMP**

**FIG. 5 (opposite page).
METHOD OF BUILDING
UP VASE (A), FIG. 4**

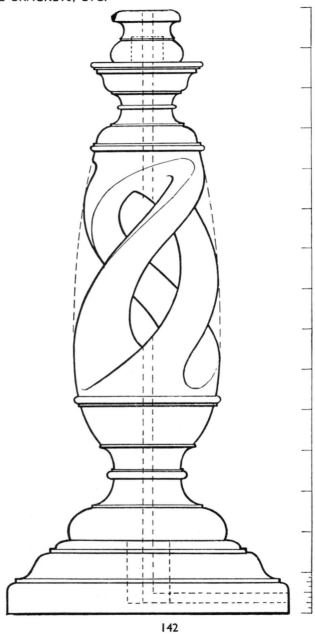

142

used to enable the boring auger to be passed in. The rest of the work is a simple between-centres turning operation. Although gouge and chisel can be used in all preliminary shaping, scraping tools are needed for most of the fine detail. When this has been completed the spiral can be marked out with a strip of thin card bent spiral-wise around the shape. The positions are stepped round at top and bottom and the card held against the marks.

Carving tools are used for cutting the spiral, and it will be found convenient to hold the work between centres in the lathe during the carving. As the cuts are deepened it will be found that they run one into the other. Rasp and file follow carving tools, and finally scraper and glasspaper.

The base is separate from the column and is joined by a dowel turned at the bottom of the latter. A disc of sycamore is sandwiched between the two, giving the effect shown in the photograph. At the top is a dish of sycamore. This needs to have a centre hole large enough to enable it to pass over the sconce. This is larger than the neck, but the difficulty is overcome by turning a small ring, cutting this in two with a chisel and slipping it in.

CHESSMEN

For best results these should be turned in a dense hardwood. Boxwood and ebony are commonly used, but such woods as African blackwood, cocus, partridge wood, rosewood, purple heart, are excellent for the black pieces. The medium weight woods can also be used if the pieces are weighted at the bottom; such woods as mahogany, teak. For the white pieces satinwood, sycamore, and holly are alternatives. Make sure before starting that there is enough wood to complete the set.

It is a help if the wood is reduced to a convenient size at the start. Thus, assuming that the pawns finish $1\frac{1}{4}$ in. diameter at the base, a length of wood can be turned to, say, $1\frac{3}{8}$ in. between centres. It can be cut up into short lengths and knocked into a hole in a wood block held in the cup chuck. This means that the lengths must be sufficient to allow for this chucking. A rough and full approximation of the shape can be turned with a small gouge. If pencil marks are made on the tool rest a narrow chisel can be used to size certain parts. Calipers can be set, but to save constant re-setting it is

FIG. 6 (opposite page). TURNED LAMP WITH CARVED TWIST

INCHES

144

better to make a series of gauges in plywood, plastic, or metal, and offer these to the work.

To turn the small members it is a good plan to grind scraping tools from old files and offer these to the work, thus ensuring uniformity. Do not attempt to make a tool which will finish the whole shape, however. There would be too much resistance, resulting in chattering or possibly in the wood flying out of the chuck. Furthermore, it would be impossible to take out local blemishes without cutting into the whole thing. It is better to make one tool to turn one large bead or two small ones, another for ogee shapes, and so on. Finish off with glasspaper, first medium then *flour* grade, and lastly rub wood chips of the same kind of wood on to the revolving wood. If polish is to be applied this can now be done, using a single rubber of lathe polish followed by wax.

The wood can now be parted off, and if the pieces are to be lead weighted it is necessary to reverse the wood into a special wood chuck which has a recess in it and saw cuts along the length. It is tightened by means of a Jubilee clip. The recess should be slightly undercut. Lead discs are cast to a close fit in the recess, and if tapped with a ball pene hammer will swell into the undercutting. Care must be taken to support the piece so that it is not damaged. In another way molten lead can be dropped into the recess, or the disc can be made molten with a soldering iron. Even so, it generally requires tapping lightly afterwards as the lead inclines to shrink as it cools. Afterwards the base is covered with baize. Some of the pieces require carving, and this is the final operation. Incidentally, the lower set of chessmen in Fig. 7 is more suitable for ivory as the bases are quite thin.

TORCH LAMP

Wall lamps make excellent subjects for turnery. That shown in Fig. 8 is inspired by the medieval torch. For its modern equivalent the flame is replaced by a candle lamp bulb with opaque glass lightly tinted red at the tip. The body of the torch is recessed to conceal a standard light fitting so that the bulb only is visible. A screwed brass tube is employed for securing the fitting. The bracket has a ¼ in. hole bored to lead the flex through to the wall fitting. The two parts should fit tightly together and should be finally secured by gluing.

FIG. 7 (opposite page). ALTERNATIVE DESIGNS FOR CHESSMEN

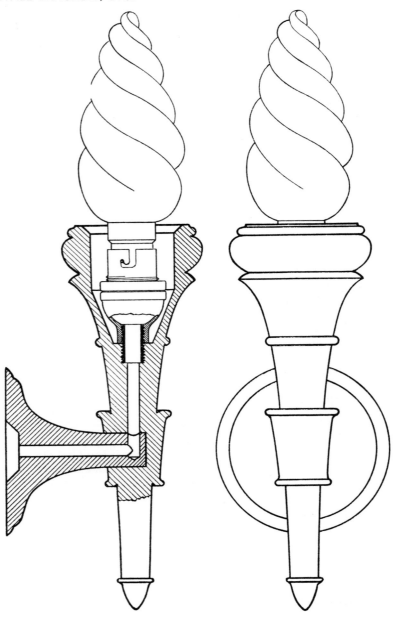

Made from hardwood this design is suitable for a polished finish or alternatively it may be painted to harmonize with an existing colour scheme. A light biscuit shade for the background with the changes in section blended in to a darker brown is one suggestion.

The simplest way of making the torch is to turn the wood to a cylinder between centres about 2 in. longer than the finished size. It is then gripped in the 3-jaw chuck or the cup chuck, and the flex hole and recess cut in at the end. A disc with spigot is turned to fit the recess, and this held at the tail stock, enabling the outer shape to be turned between centres.

The bracket is held in the cup chuck and the back recess turned. Also the flex hole. Afterwards it is mounted in a recess in a waste piece of wood screwed to the faceplate. It is held with glue with newspaper interposed. This enables the outer shape to be turned. It is necessary to cut into the waste piece to complete the shaping.

SALT AND PEPPER SHAKERS IN JARRAH AND BOX
Made by W. J. Wooldridge, Aukland

FIG. 8 (opposite page). ELECTRIC TORCH BRACKET

TERMS USED IN WOOD TURNING

Bed. The main bar or bars of a lathe to which the headstock, tailstock, and tool rest are attached. In trade lathes the bed often consists of two pieces of 9 in. by 3 in. softwood with a gap between, but the smaller proprietary lathes today have a metal bed, generally cylindrical in section.

Bell chuck. Somewhat like the cup chuck but with bolts around the periphery to enable work to be gripped.

Between centres. The method of turning in which the work is held by the fork centre at the headstock and by the ring or taper centre at the tailstock.

Bit. A boring tool usually held in the Jacobs chuck. Chief kinds are the Russell-Jennings with spur nickers; Gedge with curved cutters making nickers unnecessary; spoon with hollow along the length and scooped at the cutting end; centre, usually with screw centre; and Forstner which is guided by its circular rim rather than by its centre.

Boring auger. A long boring tool for deep holes in lamp standards, etc. Its cutting edge is set at a low angle to avoid digging in.

Bruzze. V-shaped tool used chiefly for marking out work where details are to come.

Calipers. Used to test the diameter of work being turned. For small work the spring adjustment type is the more convenient.

Centre. See under types—revolving, ring, taper.

Centreing. Process of fixing work between centres so that it runs true. It usually refers to squares, the position of which is tested by seeing whether a corner touches the rest as it is revolved by hand.

Centre punch. Punch with a conical point. Not used much in turning, but sometimes required to enable a morse drill to be started accurately.

Chisel. Usually follows the gouge. Both sides are bevelled, making an included angle of about 43 degrees. It may be ground square or at an angle. The latter is known as long-cornered. Commonly used sizes range from $\frac{1}{4}$ in. to 2 in. Both bevels should be flat, not rounded.

Chuck. See under types: cup, drill, eggcup, fork, Jacobs, screw point, three-jaw.

Chucking. The operation of fixing the work in one of the various chucks.

Cup chuck. Chuck of cup-like form. Work of irregular shape can be hammered into it.

Dividers. Sometimes needed to enable distances to be stepped around turnery, or to mark the diameter at end of work to be hollowed.

Drill. The type usually used for lathe work is the twist drill, available in a wide range of sizes. For woodwork the edges are usually ground with a slight hollow.

Drill chuck. More generally known as the Jacobs chuck (*q.v.*).

Egg-cup chuck. Chuck with bevelled screw-on ring. Wood is first turned to pass through ring but with bevelled projection at end to enable ring to grip.

Face plate. Circular plate which fits at the end of the mandrel and with screw holes at intervals. For holding wide, shallow work—bowls, platters, etc.

Fork chuck. Having short centre point and fangs at each side with intervening gaps. Also known as the prong chuck.

Forstner bit. Boring bit which is guided by its periphery rather than its centre. Gives a smooth hole.

Four-prong chuck. Similar to fork chuck but with four fangs rather than two.

Gouge. Chief types are half-round, deep which is of U section, and shallow which is seldom needed. May be normal or long-and-strong which is heavily built. Edge may be ground straight across (square) or may be nose ground, centre projecting more than sides. Bevel should be flat. Widths range from $\frac{1}{4}$ in. up to 2 in.

Headstock. The main casting at the left hand of a lathe in which the mandrel or spindle revolves.

Jacobs chuck. To hold bits and drills. Size is known by the largest diameter it will take: $\frac{1}{4}$ in., $\frac{3}{8}$ in., $\frac{1}{2}$ in. Usually with Morse taper to fit into mandrel.

Jig. Any built-up device to hold either the work or the tool to enable exact cutting or boring to be done.

L. & S. gouge. Long and strong turning gouge, heavily built and rather longer than normal.

Long-cornered chisel. Turning chisel with the edge ground at an angle.

Mandrel. The main spindle revolving in the headstock. It is usually hollow and often with Morse taper to hold various chucks. Nose is also threaded to hold face plate and certain chucks. The hollow spindle in the tailstock is also referred to as a mandrel.

Morse taper. Recognised standard taper. Mandrel often has taper to receive various chucks with Morse taper fixing.

Parting tool. Narrow, deep tool slightly splayed at the cutting edge so that it does not bind as it sinks deeply into the work.

Prong chuck. Alternative name for the fork chuck.

Pummel. The square portions left in table, chair, and stool legs to receive the rails.

Rest. Support for the tool. Short ones usually of T shape, but for long work a wood bar with rounded top edge is preferable.

Revolving centre. Pointed centre fixed to the tailstock which revolves with the work.

Ribbing. A sort of rough spiral often found when turning long work liable to whip. Can be avoided by fitting a steady, using point only of chisel the edge of which is at an angle to give a slicing cut, or by altering the speed of the lathe.

Ring centre. Back centre with small centre point and ring with flat between.

Round-nose scraper. Scraper tool with rounded end for turning hollows.

Scraping tools. Used chiefly for hard woods. Usually held radially to the work with cutting end slightly lower to avoid digging in. Generally made from old files with serrations ground away.

Screw-point chuck. Having small flat plate with centre screw. Enables small items—eggcups, small bowls, etc.—to be held.

Skew chisel. Alternative name for the long-cornered chisel.

Spigot. A projection with shoulder turned at the end of work to fit into a corresponding hole in another part.

Spoon bit. Hollowed along its length and with cutting end rounded and scooped. Not liable to wander with the grain.

Tailstock. Main casting to the right of the lathe bed in which the dead or stationary mandrel is fitted.

Taper centre. Back centre of conical form fitted in the tailstock mandrel.

Three-jaw chuck. Self-centreing chuck with double set of jaws, inside and outside. The jaws move simultaneously by the operation of a key.

Ticketer. Steel rod about $\frac{1}{4}$ in. diam. with handle. Used to turn the edge of scraping tools after sharpening. Not necessary on all woods.

Twist bit. Spiral bit with various forms of head, chief of which are Russell-Jennings and Gedge (see bit). For holding in the chuck the shank is round.

Twist drill. See Drill.

INDEX

INDEX